My Friendship
with
Saint Elizabeth Ann Seton

Other books by
Dr. Mary Hilaire (aka Sally Lynne) Tavenner:

Nun of This and Nun of That: Book One, Beginnings
(Convent Life in the 1960's)

Nun of This and Nun of That: Book Two, Making Vows
(Convent Life in the 1960's . . . the sequel.)

A Portrait of Helen Steiner Rice: A Lorain Version

France, 1996: Memoirs of a Writer in France

Peru, 2002: Memoirs of a Writer in Peru

Memories of Mom: They Called her "Dutch"
(A biography of Mary Catherine Tavenner, written by her daughter)

My Friendship
with
Saint Elizabeth Ann Seton

Mary Hilaire (Sally) Tavenner, Ph.D.

Cover art by Ciotti. Distributed freely at the Canonization of
St. Elizabeth Ann Seton.

This book was printed in the United States of America.
Let this be published to the glory of God.

Dutch Ink
www.DutchInk.com

To order additional copies of this book, contact:
Xlibris Corporation
1-888-795-4274
www.Xlibris.com
Orders@Xlibris.com or
Dutch Ink Publishing at
www.dutchink.com, www.dutchink@aol.com
1 (440) 288-0416
49331

CONTENTS

PHOTOGRAPHS

SPECIAL THANKS TO

Ann Somplack, copy-editor
Martha McGuckin, proofreader
Dr. Roy Church, President of Lorain County Community College
Robert and Mary Tavenner, my brother and sister-in-law
Ann Hageman of Tampa, Florida, benefactor
The Daughters and Sisters of Charity, Emmitsburg (1809), New York (1817),
Cincinnati (1829), Halifax (1849), Convent Station (1859), Greensburg (1870).
Particular gratitude to the following sisters who read my manuscript and
shared important information:
Sr. Betty Ann McNeil, Emmitsburg Provincial Archivist
Sr. Regina Bechtle, New York City Archivist
Sr. Judith Metz, Cincinnati Archivist

DEDICATION

To all of the Saints . . . . Especially all my loved ones on the Other Side, and to Mrs. Seton, Mother Teresa of Calcutta, St. Francis of Assisi and his good friend, QUENTIN LUKE TAVENNER, my nephew: 1979-2008.

INTRODUCTION

Dear Reader,

One of the universals in our collective lives is the need for friends. We look for them throughout our days, during every phase of our journey. I am almost 60 now, and fully understand I could not have accomplished much of anything without those who loved, enjoyed, supported, encouraged and accompanied me during my life. What may or may not seem strange is that I have also looked to those who have gone before me for companionship.

I first embraced the saints as a child. It is a fundamental precept of the Christian and Catholic faith to believe in the Communion of Saints. We believe that for those who live in God's holy realm, life has not ended, but merely changed. They eternally enjoy the benefits of Heaven. They live without fear of suffering, injustice, or longings of any kind. They live in the complete experience of God's perfect love, and yet are not indifferent to our human condition.

The saints know what it was/is like to live on Earth, with all our circumstances. They bore the burdens of their own particular times, and their examples of courage, hope, and perseverance remain as beacons of light in our darkness. All of us need inspiration. All of us need good example. Not everyone is willing to provide as much. Thank God for God. Jesus is the example we need.

I want to tell you about a friendship I have enjoyed for nearly 40 years. What makes this story unique is that my friend was born in 1774 and died in 1821. Elizabeth Ann Bayley and I had little in common. We both enjoyed some French ancestry; her mother and my mother had the same name, Catherine, and both of us worried for the eternal well-being of our fathers' souls. We both spent a number of years in religious life. We both love God first.

I hope you will enjoy some of these life adventures I have experienced because of my friendship with Saint Elizabeth Ann Seton.

CHAPTER ONE

The Circle of Oaks

Mother walked out of her bedroom, tethered to her oxygen compressor, just waking from her nap. "Sally, I just had a dream that when you write your book about Mother Seton you should begin your story with the Circle of Oaks." I was watching television in the living room at the time and her words were most welcome. First, because I thought it was a wonderful way to begin my book about St. Elizabeth Ann Seton, and second, that Mother would have the confidence in me that I would and could write such a book. That was probably about 13 years ago.

Back in 1971, I was working at Catholic University in Washington, DC on my BA in Education. Sr. Mary Ruth Morrill, a Daughter of Charity in Emmitsburg, had driven me to the Shrine of St. Elizabeth Ann Seton. Sister lived at Providence Hospital, not far from me. She needed to transport one of her sisters to the Provincial House and invited me along for the ride.

Sr. Mary Ruth was a friend to the archivist, Sr. John Mary, and on a dreary wet summer day the three of us sat in a station wagon as Sr. John Mary shared her story of the Circle of Oaks.

"Less than two hundred years before our Mother Seton ever came to this valley, there is the legend of a certain Indian chief. His name was Ottawanta. He and other Indians had been converted by the "blackrobes", the priests.

"Chief Ottawanta migrated to the banks of the Monocacy River and settled near Toms Creek. He spent most of his time in quiet seclusion raising corn and melons, searching the forests for game or the streams for fish. He had kept one particular practice of his conversion, that of praying the rosary. The priests had nurtured a strong piety to the Mother of God within the Indian, and even after religious dissension had dispersed the good missionaries, Ottawanta continued his devotion to Mary ever more fervently.

"He had been blessed with a wonderful wife, five sons and a daughter. Their family life had been rich, and Ottawanta gave credit for their protection to the Mother of Jesus. Daily, he had the custom of assembling his family to recite the fifty aves in her honor. Ottawanta also would journey to a mound just above Toms Creek to pray his rosary, to give thanks and meditate. The sight before us, this large clump of oak trees, is where he was said to have prayed."

We were parked in front of the Circle of Oaks and because of the light rain, the three of us remained in the car and looked to the mound Sister so indicated, just before us. I could feel the fervor with which she spoke.

"After a lifetime of nearly 60 years, Ottawanta had endured the sorrow of burying his wife and each of his children. He had chosen this particular place to bury them. After placing each body within the earth, he placed an acorn at the foot of the body, and another just above the head. As the years passed he fashioned a circle of his loved ones, placing them tenderly next to each other.

"Over the years the acorns flourished into trees, creating a circle within a circle of oaks, separated by the space of his family's remains. In his old age Ottawanta continued to visit this sacred burial place to diligently implore the Blessed Mother to give him a pledge of her love. He longed for her compassion and the comfort of her eternal goodness.

"One particular day, the first day of May, Ottawanta spent the entire day in prayer. Within the evening hour there appeared before the old man the Queen of Heaven with her divine Infant in her arms. She told him, 'I have heard your prayer and the many fervent aves repeated upon this very place. Soon you will join your children and your wife, far above the skies, but this spot will ever bear testimony to the love and fidelity you have for me.'"

Now it seemed as if Sr. John Mary's voice changed. It was more dramatic and took on a tone of great importance.

"Our Lady told him of the many changes to come. She told him of a woman who would bring to the valley a sisterhood. We believe she was speaking of our Mother Foundress, Mother Seton. Our Lady went on to say that these very souls, consecrated to the Lamb, will come to this very place to chant her praises. They will know her as "the flower of the field, and the lily of the valley". I was taken aback by such lovely titles. They seemed most fitting and easily embraced by the native Indian who had such love and respect for all of nature.

Sister continued. "Our Lady also spoke of men on the hillside who would serve the God Creator. And from this hillside would ring forth her praises daily." Sister went on to explain that on the mountainside there is a seminary (Mt. St. Mary's) and that the Pangborn Memorial chimes both the Angeles and rings out a carillon of songs in honor of Our Lady.

"This good Indian had received the prophecy of Mother Seton's coming, and the thousands of men and women both upon the mountain and in this valley who would faithfully love and serve the holy will of God. To this day, we refer to this vision as "the flower of the field and the lily of the valley." After Our Lady foretold the coming of our holy foundress and shared her words of comfort, she vanished.

"Within the week, Ottawanta fell ill. A missionary from Canada had come for his yearly visit to this area. He listened to the old Indian Chieftain relay the tale of his vision and the message given by the beautiful woman with the child. After giving him the final blessing, the missionary witnessed the death of the great chief, and buried him beside his family within the Circle of Oaks before us."

By now the rain had turned into a mist-like drizzle and we were free to leave the car. We walked through a metallic arch supported securely by two column-like poles. The words read, "I am the Flower of the Field and the Lily of the Valley." Just beyond this you could see the bronze statue of Our Lady of Grace, brought from Paris, France, in 1900. Placed upon a cement pedestal, the image was said to be where the vision of Mary had appeared several hundred years before. Around the statue there was a clear pattern of oak trees placed in a circle, and then another beyond the first. The trees stood tall and towered above the surrounding woods.

Sister continued, "For more years than I can recall, the sisters would come to this very place and sing their vespers, pray the rosary, and praise our Holy Mother. The more famous our beloved Mother Seton becomes, the less privacy the sisters seem to have. For generations only the sisters would come here to pray, but now, more and more pilgrims are lay people." Sister seemed a bit saddened by so many of the changes.

The three of us took time for silent prayer. It was easy to absorb the quietude and serenity upon this mound of oak trees. There was an air of sacredness, a holy solitude. My new friend, Sr. Mary Ruth, bent down to pick up an acorn, and placed it in my hand, and as we walked away that first time from the Circle of Oaks, I knew I was being given the promise of a new hope.

Though this story was first given to me as more fact than legend, I found it to be such a source of inspiration that over the years I shared the story with my mother, my friends and students. I brought many of them to this little patch of earth, hallowed by the burial and prayers of holy souls. It wasn't until I began to write this book in 2007, thirty-seven years later, that I learned this story was composed by a student while in St. Joseph's Academy in Emmitsburg, Maryland. Mary Elizabeth Smith, born in Opelousas, Louisiana on August 23, 1813, attended the Academy in 1822 and entered the Sisters of Charity on May 1, 1830. Upon entering the community she was given the name Sr. Mary Raphael and eventually became the Directress of St. Joseph's Academy in 1847. Sister died on March 2, 1884.

Circle of Oaks, Emmitsburg, MD, circa 1976.
Sr. Mary Hilaire to the right of statue.

And even though the tale of Ottawanta is a fantasy story, written by a pupil and not a proven historic event, it is, nevertheless, a true legend.

As for Sr. John Mary, I only know that she has died. She had been from the Emmitsburg area and spoke her story with such a confidence that I thought it completely true.

Much has changed since I first came to the Circle of Oaks. This particular site was sold with nearly half of the shrine grounds to the United States Government in 1979. Sister Mary Clare Hughes was the Provincial at the time. This area is now used as a National Fire and Emergency Training Center. With their permission you may visit the Circle of Oaks, and believe what you may.

To my knowledge the Circle of Oaks has never been excavated. Personally, I don't care what truth or fiction lies within Sister John Mary's tale of passion, prayer and prophecy. I only know it was one measure more to strengthening my friendship with Mrs. Seton.

As for the statue of Our Lady of Grace, brought from Paris in 1900, it was relocated in 1982, perhaps a half-mile away from the Circle of Oaks, near the wooded area behind Sacred Heart Cemetery. Interestingly there is a similar spirit of prayerful serenity in this second location, which the sisters call "Our Lady of the Field."

CHAPTER TWO

How it all Began

I was 22 years old and had entered the Sisters of St. Francis of Syracuse, New York, convent at the age of 17. I was spending my first summer at Catholic University in Washington DC, matriculating for a BA (Bachelor of Arts) in Education. My AA (Associate of Arts) in Liberal Arts was earned at our junior college, Maria Regina, in Syracuse, since closed. That summer remains memorable for many reasons; paramount among them, it was the first I had ever learned of Elizabeth Ann Seton.

Our sisters, twenty-some of us, lived in a house of studies on Varnum Campus, not far from Catholic University. They called the place Duns Scotus, in honor of a Franciscan Doctor of the Church. There were numerous houses of study in the area. From the main campus a bus came routinely to get students from our area. On one of those earliest of trips I boarded the bus and chose to sit next to a sister in a habit I did not recognize. She was a nurse and a Daughter of Charity. She lived at Providence Hospital, not far from us. She was also a student at Catholic U.

As we rode to the main campus together we talked shop. That's what nuns frequently did when they met. We would share information about our respective founders or foundresses; we talked about our history, perhaps our ministry, or where we worked. I told her about our Mother Marianne who worked on Molokai, caring for the lepers back in the late 1800's, and that our order was started by Bishop John Neumann of Philadelphia and that most of our sisters either taught or nursed. She spoke of her foundress, Mother Seton, who had been married and had five children.

I had never heard of such a thing. How does a nun marry and have children? I was immediately interested in knowing more. Soon, our commute had ended and Sr. Mary Ruth got off the bus for her class. I continued a bit further, but as luck would have it, the following day or so we met again in Mullen Library.

We continued our conversation, and Sister, knowing I was most curious, told me that she would get a book for me to read. Within a week she presented me with a biography of Mother Seton written by Fr. Joseph Dirvin, CM, a Vincentian priest. I received the book on a Friday and finished it before Sunday evening. Within the weekend I had consumed a nearly 500-page book.

The nuns in my convent took notice. Anyone who knew me knew I was not the type of person to spend a weekend alone in my bedroom reading! I noticed as well. That biography was the most powerful biography I had ever read. I remember laughing aloud, and crying too. I could see the hand of God in this person's life ever so clearly. It was a most inspirational story, and it changed me.

I wanted to live such an inspiring life. I wanted God to use me as God guided Elizabeth Ann Bayley Seton. I was mesmerized. Something else that happened was a strong attraction and affection for the nun who had loaned me this book, *Mrs. Seton*, but that's another story.

Sr. Mary Ruth realized she had planted a seed within me, and several weeks later invited me to Emmitsburg on pilgrimage. She wanted to show me many of the sites there related to Mother Seton's life. Sister needed to deliver another nun to their Provincial House in Emmitsburg, and I was invited to ride along with them.

First we visited the Provincial House, where we parted company with the other sister. Mary Ruth and I went to the Shrine Chapel to visit the remains of Mrs. Seton. Her relics were kept in a bronze and silver casket just in front of the Mother Seton side altar. I had to laugh at my first sensations as the little casket holding her relics was only several feet in length, yet I knew Mother Seton to have been about five feet tall. How could I not have expected the coffin to be a collection of bones and not contain her entire skeleton intact? It was laughable, but only for a moment, as the beauty and reverence of the altar immediately captured my attention.

In the front of this spectacular edifice, the Seton Shrine, was a likeness of St. Catherine Laboure receiving a vision of Our Lady in Paris, France, 1830. During my novitiate in Syracuse I had read the story of the Miraculous Medal and was delighted to make that connection to Mother Seton. The spiritual daughters of Mother Seton in Emmitsburg had joined St. Vincent de Paul's Daughters of Charity in France after Mother Seton's death.

Next we went to a building where we watched a slide presentation on the life of Mother Seton, especially her life in Emmitsburg. Then Sr. Mary Ruth began the process of walking me to the Stone House, the first convent in the valley. We listened to the docent explain the history of the house. At that time, the Stone House rested upon its original site, not far from Toms Creek. After the selling of the sisters' property to the US Government, the building was moved to its present location, across from the Provincial House.

White House. Where Mrs. Seton died on January 4, 1821.
Considered the "Cradle of Catholic Education" in the United States.
Photo by Tanya A. Geilser, circa 1978.

When we walked into the White House, a building Mother Seton had named St. Joseph's House, and the second convent in the valley, built during the winter of 1809, I had a most extraordinary experience. Sister and I were standing in the room where Mother Seton had died. The docent had already explained much of the history of the house, considered by some to be the first free Catholic school and the cradle of the Catholic school system in America.

As we remained in the room I felt as if my very soul had opened, and from above there poured an abundance of grace and energy, filling my very essence. I felt tears of joy and could not speak. Sr. Mary Ruth noticed the tears but turned away, not prying. Even if she had inquired I could not have explained. From there we continued on to visit the Mortuary Chapel and community cemetery, where two of Mother Seton's daughters are buried, not far from the White House.

Later, we met with Sr. John Mary, the community archivist, who accompanied us to the Circle of Oaks. There was a mist of rain, and here Sister shared the legend of Chief Ottawanta and the prophecy of Mother Seton's coming to St. Joseph's Valley. But Sr. Mary Ruth was not finished with me yet. Now, before returning to Washington DC, we drove several miles over and onto Mount St. Mary's. Here she showed me where Mother Seton's son, William, was buried with some of his family members. We walked the asphalt path up toward one of the oldest American replicas of the Lourdes France Shrine, the Grotto.

Here Mother Seton came regularly to teach religion to the mountain children, for Sunday mass, and to find a source of peace and spiritual nourishment. Looking back on that day I can so easily recall many of the impressions. By the time we walked the mountain path, the sun had returned and the smells of surrounding plant life filled the air.

I was especially pleased to see the statue of St. Francis in front of Corpus Christi Stone Chapel. Coming from a Franciscan tradition, finding a likeness of Francis here made me feel even more at home. Inside the chapel the Eucharist was contained in a monstrance. Not far from there was a reservoir and in the center, a statue similar to one in Lourdes. We walked the Rosary path back to the parking lot and explored the grounds in front of the 95-foot pedestal supporting a 25-foot gold-leafed bronze figure of Our Lady of Grace, known as Pangborn Memorial.

It was all so beautiful and I think that day was, by far, the most inspiring I ever spent with the woman who first introduced me to Elizabeth Ann Seton.

CHAPTER THREE

The Following Five Years

After that first summer in DC at Catholic University, when I first "met" Mother Seton, I returned to teach at Assumption in Syracuse. I remember being very enthusiastic about teaching the children the life of Mrs. Seton, and did all I could to foster devotion to her. I also taught religion class for Sr. Celestine at Holy Trinity Parish, and one day she gave me a lovely foot-tall statue of Mother Seton. I so appreciated her gift, and treasure the statue still proudly displayed in my bedroom, to this day. The following year I returned to Catholic University, and Sr. Mary Ruth was kind enough to act as a guide on our minibus, "Brother Caritas. I had coaxed our sisters to visit the Shrine of St. Elizabeth Ann Seton.

What was somewhat ironic was that I could not get the sisters I lived with very interested in Mother Seton, but when I told them that Gettysburg, PA, was only about ten miles down the road, and after visiting the Shrine they could tour Gettysburg, they agreed to go. The nuns filled the minibus and later confided that they enjoyed the Shrine as much, if not more, than Gettysburg.

However, after that second summer Sr. Mary Ruth decided to distance herself from me. When I returned to New York she wrote me asking that we no longer have any further contact. She did not explain why, only asking that I destroy any letters she may have given me and dispose of any small exchanges we may have made. By now I was teaching in Fulton, New York.

I respected Mary Ruth's wishes but understood nothing. Over the next few years I continued to take sisters to Emmitsburg during my summer studies and learn more of Mother Seton. I was beginning to give talks on her life to students and parish groups. People were starting to look at me as somewhat of an authority on Mrs. Seton. My devotion to her continued to grow in leaps and bounds, but my disconnect with Mary Ruth also continued until one summer when I accidentally met her at the shrine. She just happened to be there when I was.

We spoke in one of the Provincial House parlors. The good news was that she gave me permission to write her again, never explaining her previous need for separation. I just accepted the fact that we could communicate again.

The Mortuary Chapel. Mother Seton called this cemetery, "God's Little Acre". [See final footnote on last page.] The chapel was built with a substantial donation from her son, William, after his mother's death. Mrs. Seton's body was first buried several yards to the right of the Mortuary Chapel, then in 1846, placed in the Mortuary Chapel. Her body was exhumed from here in 1962. Currently her remains are located at the Seton Shrine Altar. Archbishop James Roosevelt Bayley, her nephew, and Bishop John McNamara, Auxiliary Bishop of Washington, DC are now interred within this chapel. Photo was taken in 1983.

During the summers, on certain Sundays, I persuaded our sisters at Duns Scotus to visit Providence Hospital. We would go to mass there and I would plan the liturgy. The hospital chapel had a television camera so that mass could be seen by patients in their rooms. Sr. Monica Coffay, Daughter of Charity, was in charge of the camera and always appreciated our coming. I recall the last time I visited with Sr. Monica, just before I finished my studies at Catholic University. She said to me, "Sister, I know you love our holy foundress so very much. I am going to pray that someday you are able to attend her canonization."

I had never even conceived such an idea. Where would it be held? In Italy? In the United States? And when would it happen? Truthfully, I did not anticipate being alive when she was canonized, because the process sometimes involves hundreds of years. However I was deeply touched that she could see how much I loved Elizabeth Seton and I so embraced her beautiful thought.

In September of 1974, I was transferred from teaching in Fulton, NY, to Albany, NY. At the beginning of the school year I attended a 200th anniversary mass of Mother Seton's birth, celebrated in the Albany diocesan cathedral. There I met a group of her spiritual daughters, Daughters of Charity, who taught at Cardinal McClosky High School. Sr. Sylvia Borden was close to my age, and she invited me to their convent after the mass for a meal with the sisters. That was the beginning of a treasured Mrs. Seton relationship that continues to this day. Sr. Sylvia helped me so much to survive my year in Albany. She left the convent shortly before I did in 1984, and over the years we have remained friends.

I had made my Final Profession the summer before moving to Albany and had received some gift money from family and friends. My superior could not understand why I wanted to use my gift money to visit New York City. She said, "I could understand if you wanted to see Yankee Stadium or the Empire State Building!" No, I wanted to visit historical sites related to Mother Seton. I was given permission to take the bus and stay at one of our convents in Hoboken, New Jersey. It was a most memorable and inspiring weekend.

I remember visiting the New York Motherhouse for the Sisters of Charity and meeting with the archivist. I also visited a hospital run by the Sisters. I went to see Trinity Episcopal Church, where Mother Seton's family had worshipped. I went to St. Peter's and the nuns in that parish at the time invited me for a meal. I especially recall visiting Mrs. Seton's home on State Street, now Holy Rosary Church. I did most of it alone, but one of our sisters, Sr. Patricia, joined me one afternoon. She wanted us to go to Covenant House, a home for troubled youth that our sisters used to staff. We did that too. I took this weekend trip around October, as I remember the colorful foliage.

In late winter of 1975, I received a letter from Sr. Lorraine, a Franciscan sister from Massachusetts. I had met Sr. Lorraine when I taught at Assumption in Syracuse, New York, and she was missioned at Our Lady of Pompeii School. Sister wrote to tell me that Blessed Elizabeth Ann Seton was to be canonized and to become Saint Elizabeth Ann Seton in Rome on September 14, 1975. That was only months away! I could hardly believe the news. Upon reading her words, my spirit filled with a Te Deum of gratitude and utter joy! I literally went to my knees in gratitude.

That spring, at Eastertime I was at the Franciscan Motherhouse in Syracuse for my annual retreat and decided to do something unimaginable. I don't know how I ever found the courage, but I called our Reverend Mother General, Mother Viola, on the phone and asked for an appointment. I wanted to sit with Mother in person to explain my devotion to Mrs. Seton and to ask if there was any possible way I might be able to go to Italy for this most historical event. Mother Viola was too busy to see me for an appointment, as she was packing for visitation in Hawaii, and asked on the phone, "What is it that you need, Sister?"

I hesitated because I did not want to ask for such a monumental permission on the phone. I had no choice. I needed to verbalize my request then and there.

"Mother, you know I have been a student of Mother Seton's life for the past four years. I never expected to even be alive for her canonization as the process sometimes will span centuries, but do you think there might be some way I could possibly go to Rome in September to attend the canonization of America's first native-born saint?"

There was no hesitation. I had no idea what to expect. She replied, "Why, yes, Sister, that can be arranged. I would like to have gone myself, but I am scheduled for a trip to our mission in Puerto Rico at that time, so I will send you to Rome to represent myself and our community."

Was I shocked? To say the least. I was also higher than a kite, and when I hung up, the first nun I encountered was Sister E. I could not contain my excitement and wanted to share what had just transpired. When I told Sr. E my news she replied, "You really think you are coming up in community now, don't you? Going to Rome! You think you are quite important now!"

What? I did not think that at all. Such an idea never came to mind. In fact I went from feeling high as a kite to kicked in the gut, if you can imagine. I knew that I loved Mrs. Seton as one loves a best friend and I that was going to have the privilege of being at an event I had long hoped and prayed would happen. In that moment I was not considering myself at all important . . . just very, very, very fortunate. Sr. E took the wind from my sails, but she could not dampen my resolve to experience the opportunity of a lifetime, with the profoundest of anticipation and gratitude!

When I told Sr. Consolata, one of my formation directors and my superior at Duns Scotus House of Studies in Washington, that I had received permission to attend Mother Seton's Canonization in Rome, Italy, she also had news for me. She told me that my friend, Sr. Monica Coffay, had died unexpectedly. I was stunned. Then Sr. Consolata told me the very date Sr. Monica had been buried was the very same day I had received permission to attend the canonization.

So the next chapter of this book will be about my first trip to Italy. Nine days: Sept 11th until Sept 19th, 1975. I had kept a journal of that visit and even published a version of it for the Syracuse sisters.

CHAPTER FOUR

The Canonization

More than 40 years ago, on Wednesday, September 11th, 1975, I left the Syracuse Hancock Airport to catch a Mother Seton Guild chartered flight at JFK International Airport, in New York City. On board were 170 Mother Seton Guild members. Annabelle Melville, a famed biographer of St. Elizabeth Ann Seton, was on the plane and I was thrilled to make her acquaintance, having previously read the biography, *Elizabeth Bayley Seton*, which she had written. Annabelle was honored to be the second occupant of the Catholic University's Chair of American Catholic Church History. (Six years later I would meet another famous biographer of St. Elizabeth Ann Seton—Father Joseph Dirvin. We met when I served as a consultant for a 3 million dollar movie about Mother Seton's life, entitled "A Time for Miracles". The movie was based on his book, *Mrs. Seton*. This was my introduction to Mother Seton's life. Both of these famed biographers are now deceased.)

At JFK International I met two Immaculate Heart of Mary nuns, Sr. Elizabeth Seton and her companion, Sr. Marita Edward. Sr. Seton's parish had paid for the two trips to Rome and the two sisters were very good friends. Sr. Seton was probably in her 40's and Sr. Marita was closer to my age. We were all giddy with anticipation of our coming adventures.

Upon arrival, Sr. Antoinette, one of our sisters in Rome, greeted me in the airport, then we went to our convent. I remember the traffic was fast and furious, much different than driving in the United States. Our Franciscan convent was actually a hotel just outside the walls of the Vatican. In Rome, religious hotels are called hospices or pilgrim houses. These are places for the pilgrim tourists to sleep and eat; our sisters missioned there literally earned their incomes from cleaning, cooking, and doing laundry for the guests.

The Syracuse Franciscan Convent hospice in Rome where Sr. Mary Hilaire stayed while attending the canonization, 1975. Via Nicolo V. 35. The building has since been sold.

I had not slept on the plane and even though I had been awake for more than 20 hours, I had enough energy to walk over to St. Peter's Basilica and explore for another six hours before I returned to our convent. I slept soundly for the following 14 hours! This was because of the jet lag effect. I came to Italy for one purpose: to attend the canonization of America's first native born saint, Elizabeth Ann Bayley Seton. 14,000 Americans ventured to Rome to attend her canonization. I was one of them. Most of the Americans in attendance were elderly, and I was definitely one of the youngest to be there.

Every 25 years, traditionally, Rome declares a Holy Year, with special spiritual benefits for visiting pilgrims. 1975 was proclaimed a Holy Year.

September 12th: Friday

On the morning of September 12th (two days before the canonization), I awoke for a meager breakfast and began my own tour of Rome's four major basilicas: St. Peter's, St. Mary Major, St. John Lateran, and St. Paul's Outside the Walls. Scheduled busses conveniently transported Holy Year pilgrims throughout the sites of Rome and to scheduled activities related to the canonization.

I had just come out of St. Mary Major Basilica and literally tripped on a step, falling into the arms of Sr. Patricia Borders, a Sister of Providence from Indiana, and her brother Chuck. Sister asked who I was and when she learned I was in Rome alone she asked that I join her and her brother for lunch. Eager as I was to visit the next basilica, I decided to join them. It was during lunch that I learned Sr. Patricia and Chuck's brother was the Archbishop of Baltimore! Archbishop William Borders was certainly one of the most esteemed pilgrims in Rome for the canonization because of the year Mother Seton had lived in Baltimore and the fact that his predecessor, Bishop John Carroll, had been the one to bring Mother Seton to Maryland.

It was a lovely visit during lunch and then I continued my pilgrimage to the other three basilicas. Another clear memory I had that day was at St. Paul's Outside the Walls. There was a rose garden, and inside the bloom of a pink rose I discovered a very small gold colored key. I thought it very strange and gave the discovery some personal significance. I thought I should give it to Sr. Antonia Legnetto, my superior in Syracuse at Holy Trinity School at the time, as I thought it might mean she would become a Mother General of the community someday. It was a very full day.

September 13th: Saturday

The day before the canonization I visited the Secretariat, an office in Rome designated for the purpose of distributing reserved tickets, selling relics, medals, etc. I walked to the Secretariat, and on the way, I met two very excited women who introduced themselves as Francesca Quaratesi and her sister, Giovanna, the great great granddaughters of Antonio and Amabilia Filicchi!

When Mr. and Mrs. Seton were experiencing a serious reverse of fortune, and when Elizabeth's husband's health had failed, it was decided that they would go to Livorno, Italy. There, William Seton, Elizabeth's husband, had business associates and good friends, the Filicchi family. It was the Filicchis who did all in their power to help the Setons, especially after William had died in Italy. The Filicchi influence led Elizabeth to convert from her Protestant Episcopal faith to Catholicism.

For no reason apparent to me, two living direct descendants of Antonio and Amabilia Filicchi had approached me and introduced themselves. I knew exactly who they were but was totally surprised that they would just stop and talk with me as we passed in the street. I could feel their excitement and anticipation for what was to happen the next day. That particular memory has remained indelible in my mind.

[During my second trip to Rome thirty years later, in 2005 to attend the Beatification of Mother Marianne of Molokai, I had returned to Livorno and was visiting St. Elizabeth Ann Seton Church. Francesca Quaratesi, was "coincidentally" visiting the parish at the same time. She invited my sister-in-law, Sadie, and me to visit with her the following day at her home in Pisa, about 10 miles from the church. We were invited for dinner. We went and that, too, was an extraordinary experience. Francesca was a perfect hostess, showing us the building where William Magee Seton had died back in 1803, a house just across from Chapel de la Spina. That second serendipitous encounter with a Filicchi descendent was a particular grace, and much more than coincidental.

In a later chapter I will give you a brief biography of Elizabeth Seton's life, and you will better understand the important contributions of the Filicchi family. If you are well versed in the life of Mrs. Seton, then you clearly understand these amazing privileges, to have accidentally met Francesca twice in Italy.]

I remained in the Secretariat for several hours, visiting and purchasing mementos to take to the canonization for the Pope's blessing, then to give as gifts back home. I was told the Secretariat was distributing 15,000 tickets for those who would be given seats in the Vatican Piazza. Others would need to stand. Each pilgrim who came to get his or her reserved ticket for the canonization received a ticket and was given a portrait of Mother Seton by an Italian artist, Ciotti. This is the likeness of Mother Seton placed on the cover of this book. Pilgrims were taking one or two copies of the Ciotti portrait, but I wanted 560 so that I might give every member of our community one of the pictures!

Francesca Quaratesi, great-great-granddaughter of Antonio and Amabilia Filicchi.
Photo taken at her home in Pisa on May 23, 2005 by MHT

Sr. Mary Clare Hughs, the Provincial of the Emmitsburg Province, said I would need to speak with Fr. William Sheldon, Assistant to the Postulator General in Rome (who was originally from Baldwinsville, NY, just outside of Syracuse, and knew our community well). He was not available at the time, so I went to find a meal and returned to wait another two hours until he arrived.

When he did, he gave me a package, saying it contained 500 copies of the portrait, and I counted an additional 60 copies so that I might have enough for each of our sisters in the community. Then I returned to the hospice where I was staying and counted the pictures. There were only 200 in the bundle Father had given me, so I only had 260. I walked back to the Secretariat to get the last package of 200, now having 460, not enough for each of our sisters.

[When I returned to the United States, I brought the Ciotti portraits to Mother Viola, our Superior General, and she decided that I should distribute them, which I did. I gave them all away, but first wrote, in red ink, on the back of each: "Blessed by Pope Paul VI at the canonization of St. Elizabeth Ann Seton, 9-14-1975". Upon the image, I drew a red line in the white sleeve near her right hand, so that I might recognize and identify the prints I had personally brought back from Italy.]

September 14th: Sunday

During the night I had a most disturbing dream. Because the hospice was full of pilgrims at the time, I slept in a second floor room near the front of the convent, just above the entrance. It was where the sisters would normally socialize. I had a nightmare that night. Something (which I felt was evil) was pulling at my soul, wanting me. I fought much of the night, refusing to yield and imploring the holy of name of Jesus. I insisted, "No, I belong to Jesus!"

With the dawn of first light, the entity gave up and flew out the window. Yes, it was most vivid and obviously memorable because that was almost forty years ago.

I rose for mass with our sisters, had breakfast, and left the convent around 7:30 AM. I carried a large black suitcase filled with the 460 Ciotti portraits of Mother Seton, relics, books, medals, etc.—all of which I wanted blessed by Pope Paul during the canonization. My suitcase must have weighed between 60 and 70 pounds because I could barely drag it. Yet I was determined to take it with me.

I was not even two minutes outside of the convent, beginning a series of stone steps to a street below, when two men came from behind. One was an Episcopalian priest, Fr. Raymond Avent, and his younger friend, Roger. They were in Rome from London, England, to attend the canonization and immediately offered to assist me. We soon learned that we were both going to the Vatican Piazza, and they insisted on taking care of the suitcase. We sat together in the 6th row. We had wonderful seats and could easily watch the two living miracle cures, both Ann O'Neill Hooe and Carl Kalin, receive Eucharist from the Holy Father. Hundreds of priests filed out of St. Peter's Church to distribute communion to the 125,000-150,000 people who filled the piazza.

The joy of that celebration was inexplicable. I kept on thinking, "Now, people all over the world will come to know and love the life and example of my friend, Elizabeth Ann Bayley Seton."

After communion I opened my blue notebook and began to read the names and intentions of almost fifty people who had asked me to pray for them at the canonization. The event was televised, and one of the cameramen was perched upon a platform very close to us. When the Holy Father proclaimed to all of us, "Elizabeth Ann Bayley Seton is a saint!" the lot of us cheered and clapped. The joy was incomparable. The Pope continued, "Elizabeth Ann Bayley Seton is a Saint! Children of the Father, learn of her life, her rich example! Be edified and imitate!"

I thought it interesting that the canonization celebration would conclude with three parachute jumpers leaping from a plane and landing in the Vatican Piazza. Each carried a different flag: one for America, one for Italy and one for the papacy. They were all connected to a smoke trail, increasing their visibility. Two of them landed in the piazza but the wind blew one out of sight. The crowd was electric with excitement.

Then Fr. Raymond and Roger offered to carry my suitcase back to the convent. "You don't want to leave here yet, so let us do this for you. We saw the hospice you left and we'll leave this there for your return." I was incredibly grateful and thought to myself, "Leave it to Mrs. Seton to send Episcopalians to my rescue!"

I did stay throughout the afternoon in the piazza. On the steps of the Vatican, I taught perfect strangers about Mother Seton. Some had no idea what had transpired during the day. I remember picking up from the ground a few of the support splinters of wood from the temporary altar constructed for the canonization mass. There were also some leftover leaves from the flowers. I have safely tucked these little relics away in the attic for someone, perhaps, to find and care about.

Now a true story (from the sublime to the ridiculous). When I left the piazza around 4:30 PM, I felt radiant with joy. As I walked home a very nice looking man in an exquisite black Mercedes Benz called out to me. "My, you look happy!" I answered, "I am! Today America received her first native-born saint. Mother Seton was just canonized in the Vatican Piazza!"

He returned, "You are beautiful!" I thanked him for his compliment and decided to approach his car to share more of Mother Seton and her canonization. After listening with much interest, or so it seemed to me, he suggested we celebrate by having dinner together. He explained he was from France but that he owned a villa on the Tiber River not far from where we were.

The stranger had all the appearances of being a decent, kind man. I declined his invitation for no other reason than I was eager to return to my community and share the happiness with them. He pressed his invitation, and young trusting fool I may have been, got into his car. I still considered his offer one of honorable intentions as I had shared meals with strangers in Rome before.

He then offered me a ride to my convent so that I might "change into something more comfortable". That's when I began to feel this was not a good idea. I told him, "I wear my habit everyday. This is the only dress I wear." Then I took his hand to thank him sincerely for the invitation, but felt it better to forgo an evening meal together. I got out of the car and continued my ten minute walk back to the convent, where I dined with the sisters and bubbled with effusive joy. Certainly, a day I will never forget, among the many, many thousands lived.

September 15th: Monday

There was another Sister of St. Francis who attended the canonization of Mother Seton. Interestingly enough she was also from Lorain, Ohio! I did not know her. At the time worked in our leper colony on Molokai. Her name was Sr. Wilma. The convent superior, Sr. Ambrosia, had arranged for a driver to take the three of us and five or six lay people to Assisi for the day. We visited the Basilica of St. Francis, the Hermitage, where Francis lived and slept in a cave, the Basilica of St. Clare, where Clare's incorrupt, (but blackened by age) body lies, San Damiano Church, and the Portiuncula.

We attended mass at the Basilica of St. Francis but I stayed for another at the Portiuncula. This word means "little portion" in Italian and is the little church that St. Francis repaired and where he worshipped. Of all the places in Assisi, the Portiuncula touched me the most. It was so simple, humble and reverent a space.

During our pilgrimage I kept on thinking, "Oh, if only every Franciscan Sister could visit this holy place. How could they not be edified, inspired and renewed in faith?" It was such a profoundly simple joy to be there, and sharing the day with members of my Franciscan community, Sr. Ambrosia and Sr. Wilma, made it even more special.

September 16th: Tuesday

This day I had planned to get a train for Livorno (Leghorn), the place where Mrs. Seton's husband was buried and where she received the seeds of conversion. Unfortunately for me, there was a train strike, and I knew no other means of getting there. I decided to go to St. Peter's to pray and there I chanced to meet Sr. Isabel Toohey with a few other Daughters of Charity from Emmitsburg.

Sister Isabel was highly credited with much of the canonization proceedings and helped to plan construction of the Provincial House in Emmitsburg, now housing the relic remains of Mother Seton. Sister purchased the Italian marble used in the Shrine and Provincial House. She also had been to Livorno in 1947 to see if there were any Filicchi descendants there. Sr. Isabel discovered the two great-great-granddaughters and invited them to attend St. Joseph College, in the United States, then staffed by the sisters. (These were the same two women I had met just before the canonization, quite serendipitously.) Only Francesca decided to come to America and study with Mother Seton's religious community.

When I met Sr. Isabel I expressed my disappointment at not being able to go to Livorno. She then shared with me that she too wanted to return to Livorno. I mentioned that my superior, Sr. Ambrosia, had been able to arrange a minibus and driver for our trip to Assisi the day before, and maybe she could do the same for us, so that we might visit Livorno. Sr. Isabel offered to pay for the service, and I returned to the hospice to see if we could make these arrangements. It could be done. I returned to St. Peter's and later confirmed with Sister Isabel our arrangements to visit Livorno the following day. Then I toured the Sistine Chapel and Vatican Museums.

That evening the first of the Triduum Masses was to be celebrated at St. Paul's Outside-the-Walls. Sr. Isabel invited me to ride on the Daughter of Charity chartered bus from Santa Marta's Convent (their convent located beyond the Swiss Guards and within the Vatican walls) and to use her seat as she did not plan to attend.

The bus was overcrowded and some of the sisters needed to sit on the floor, but a dear Emmitsburg Daughter of Charity by the name of Sr. M. Francis Campbell offered me her lap and I accepted. Sr. Francis and her friend also told me they would love to join us for the trip to Livorno with Sr. Isabel and her companion, Sr. Constantia Clark. There were still five empty seats on our minibus and I wanted more people to join us, to help defray the expense for Sr. Isabel.

At this Triduum Mass, the principal celebrant was Cardinal Shehan and the homilist was Archbishop W. Borders. I sat next to Sr. Mary Alice Fowler, D.C. She was the nun who first asked Ann O'Neill Hooe's mother to pray to Mother Seton for a miracle. Mrs. O'Neill received the miracle and Ann was cured of acute lymphatic leukemia, credited to the intercession of Mother Seton. It was the first and only time I ever met Sr. Mary Alice Fowler. She was radiant and she gave me permission to take her picture. After the mass I declined a return bus ride

Sr. Mary Alice Fowler, DC. Photo was taken on September 16, 1975 at the first of the Triduum of Masses, held at St. Paul's Outside-the-Walls by Sr. Mary Hilaire Tavenner.

back to the Vatican because I wanted to find my way to the DiVinci Hotel. I knew many of the guild members were there, and I wanted to see if I could interest some of them in going to Livorno the next day. According to their schedule, it was a free day and people could take side trips of their own interest. I especially had Sr. Elizabeth Seton and her friend, Sr. Marita Edward, the Immaculate Heart of Mary nuns from Philadelphia, in mind.

I managed to find my way, stopping in a bar for help. It Italy a "bar" means it is a restaurant as well. People were very helpful, and I made the necessary bus connections successfully, using my survival Spanish skills. Upon arriving at the hotel, I first went to find the two sisters I had met in New York City when preparing to board our chartered flight. They had planned to visit Capri and could not be joining our group to Livorno. I saw Sr. Marita without her veil that evening and was amazed to discover that such a young woman had such striking white hair! Later, when I got to know Sr. Marita in Philadelphia, I learned she had treatments for cancer which nearly took her life. The chemotherapy and radiation changed the color of her hair, and even though Sr. Marita was not a documented public miracle, her cure was considered by many as miraculous.

[It seems that when Sr. Marita made her first vows in Westchester, PA, at the age of 21, she also received the last sacrament, anointed at the same ceremony. Before the ceremony had ended, she was unconscious and carried from the chapel. After this, Sister required a most serious and extensive surgery. She was not expected to survive and many attributed Marita's recovery to the relic of St. Elizabeth Ann Seton which was placed upon her by Fr. Kavanagh, brother to Sr. Elizabeth Seton, and Sr. Marita Edward's sponsor into the community. However, many people had also prayed to Blessed John Newmann, so it was not possible to determine if the restored health was the intercession of Mother Seton or John Neumann. Obviously it was the will of God.

The following year my community sent me to study at St. Charles Seminary in Philadelphia to earn a masters degree in religious studies and co-incidentally Sr. Marita both studied and later taught at the seminary. I got to know both of these sisters better, but both Sr. Marita Edward and I left our respective communities and have had no contact in many years. Sr. Elizabeth Seton has since died.]

Returning from their room, and coming down the stairway, I again met Sr. Patrice Borders! This was the same Sister of Providence that I "tripped into" on the steps of St. Mary Major Basilica. Sister was just as surprised to see me as I was to see her. She asked if I had come to attend the dinner given in honor of Cardinal Shehan and her brother, Archbishop Borders, by the Diocese of Baltimore. I told her, "I did not even know it was happening!"

"Have you eaten yet?" I told her, "No."

She immediately scooped me up by my arm and took me to her brother, "Billy, I want this young sister to stay and have supper with us. Is there an extra place for her?" He replied with a delightful twinkle in his blue eyes, "Of course we have room! Put Sister at our table. Knowing you, she will be very much at home!"

That was another extraordinary and memorable event from my first pilgrimage to Rome. After dinner the Archbishop led the 200 or so guests of the Baltimore Diocese in song. He even held the microphone for me as we all sang "When Irish Eyes are Smiling." There was the "Cheers, Cheers" song for Notre Dame and others included in our songfest that evening.

After dinner I met and spoke with Cardinal Shehan, who sat at the table next to us. Mr. and Mrs. Hooe sat as guests at the Cardinal's table. I was delighted to meet Ann O'Neill Hooe, Mother Seton's second documented miraculous cure and her husband, Robert. I had read and studied a good deal about her before our meeting.

My meeting with Ann was memorable for us both. Interestingly she remembers me as wearing a traditional habit at the time, but I had changed to the modified basic black dress and veil on August 28th, Mother Seton's birthday, less than a month before coming to Rome. We both acknowledged a profound connection at the time. Short as our first visit was, we were both determined to know each other better.

We had five more seats on the minibus for Livorno and Ann wanted to bring her mother, her sister, her husband and a friend. That would fill the van. However there were some issues that caused our lack of communication and the four Daughters of Charity and myself left early the next day without Ann and her family. Ann told me candidly, years later, that her husband, Bob, was causing an upset and it was easier not to join us.

September 17th: Wednesday

To get to Livorno, (Americans usually refer to Livorno as Leghorn, more popularly dubbed so in the 19th century, and especially so after WWII), the four Daughters of Charity, myself and the bus driver traveled five hours, stayed for five hours, and returned to Rome via another five hour ride. Dear Sister Isabel was the eldest of our group, and returned totally fatigued.

Yet Sr. Isabel was the perfect guide. She had been there before and could navigate our journey remarkably well. We visited Blessed Elizabeth Ann Seton Church, a parish in the process of planning to build Saint Elizabeth Ann Seton Church. We went to see St. Caterina Church, not far from the Filicchi former offices of business, and the Filicchi House, which had become a school for children during our visit. Part of the Filicchi House (palazzo) had been destroyed by American bombing during World War II and repaired.

Livorno, (Leghorn) Italy, at the time of canonization. Blessed Elizabeth Ann Seton Church (temporary); Filicchi House; Sanctuary of Montenero; drawing of current St. Elizabeth Seton Church; Italian artist image of Mother Seton in center.

Elizabeth's husband, William Magee Seton, actually died in a building across from the river running through Pisa. Pisa is about ten miles from Livorno. After quarantine in the Livorno Lazaretto, Mr. and Mrs. Seton and their daughter, Anna Marie, went to Pisa. Shortly after being released, William died, and Elizabeth and her daughter returned to stay at the Filicchi Palazzo in Livorno as guests of Antonio and Amabilia Filicchi.

We also went to pray at the grave of William Magee Seton, buried in a Protestant cemetery in Livorno. After the new St. Elizabeth Ann Seton Church was finished, William's body was exhumed from this cemetery and placed at the church. I recall that the cement slab/marker covering his grave had also been damaged by the bombs of the Second World War.

I will never forget our visit to the San Jacopo Lazaretto. It was a prison, more or less, for travelers who arrived by sea and were suspected of having a contagious disease. The upstairs of the structure was, when I was there, a chapel, but below the rooms were dark and dank. The upper regions were destroyed during WWII bombings.

I explored a little by myself, trying to imagine the Setons confined to such circumstances, and came across a room that was filled with the skulls and skeletal remains of people who had died in the Lazaretto. It was a startling discovery, causing me to stumble in the darkness, bruising my leg and ripping a rather large whole in my black stockings.

Our last visit before returning to Rome was to a lovely shrine upon a nearby mountain. It was called the Sanctuary of Montenero, a shrine to the Mother of God. Mother Seton made mention of her visits to this sanctuary, St. Caterina Church, and to the chapel inside of the Filicchi home, in the journal she kept while in Italy. Mother Seton recorded much of her stay for her beloved sister-in-law, Rebecca Seton, who died shortly after Elizabeth's return to New York.

September 18th: Thursday

I had only a short time left in the morning as I would be leaving for the airport after lunch. I decided to spend my final hours at St. Peter's Church. I was able to explore some of the tombs below and earlier in the week had climbed the cupola at the very top of St. Peter's. Now I came to give thanks for a week I would never forget and a privilege I will never cease appreciating.

Before returning to the United States, our charter plane stopped to refuel at Shannon Airport in Ireland. This gave the pilgrims an hour or so to shop at the Shannon airport and spend what few dollars we might have had left. During the trip home the Mother Seton Guild members socialized. I spent some pleasant time with Annabelle Melville, famed biographer of Mother Seton. I reflected over the past week, and all of the amazing events.

September 19th: Friday

We arrived at JFK International Airport shortly before midnight. The approach to our landing was rough, and we spontaneously broke into a hymn in honor of the Blessed Mother. I realized I was a little short of cash, needing a taxi to the Port Authority to get a bus for Syracuse. One of the pilgrims loaned me $10.00, but I was able to return it once I was home. I rode all night on the bus, sleeping off and on. I was not able to sleep on the plane ride back to the US, but I could sleep on the bus.

I arrived at 7:00 AM in Syracuse and called my superior, Sr. Antonia, to get me at the station. I was able to return to school in time to teach my students at Holy Trinity School that day, and I did.

CHAPTER FIVE

A Short Biography of Mrs. Seton

One of the pilgrims staying in the Franciscan Hospice in Rome for the canonization was a man by the name of Oscar Barker. He was covering the event for the Albany/Syracuse Diocesan newspapers. We met by chance that week in the hospice where we both stayed, and after the canonization he contacted me, asking if I might write a story for the newspapers about Mother Seton's life. He would pay me $100.00 plus expenses.

I asked Sr. Michael Kevin, one of our sisters, if she wanted to drive with me to Emmitsburg so I could compose the story there. I wanted Mother Seton to help me write it. Mr. Barker wanted the story to print in time for the first world celebration of Saint Elizabeth Ann Seton's feastday, January 4, 1976. They say everything is timing, and the canonization had remarkable timing . . . . it happened in 1975, The International Year of the Woman, just in time for 1976, The Bicentennial Year of the United States of America.

On December 24-31, 1975, *The Catholic Sun* in Syracuse, New York, published the following story, which I wrote at the request of Mr. Barker.

On January 4th, the universal Church will celebrate for the first time the Feast of St. Elizabeth Ann Seton, a saint for all Americans. Everyone can find in Mother Seton something of his or her own life. She was like us, and yet unlike us. She was always willing to trust God completely with the plan of her own destiny.

I write these lines in Emmitsburg, Maryland, before the remains of St. Elizabeth Ann Seton. Bone and dust seem only to remain. But what also remains is her spirit of trust, her example of fidelity, her enthusiasm to live for God alone. There remain her legacy of love, her thirst for truth and even her gentle sense of humor.

There remains also for each of us a lesson of womanliness, a goal for sanctity. There remain 7,500 of her spiritual daughters. Indeed, there remains for all the world and for all ages to come, the example of another saint . . . and for the first time, American born.

Happy Birthday, America! What better gift could the Catholic Church extend to all of us for our bicentennial? Her life speaks to us in many ways and in many guises.

Elizabeth's mother died when she was only three. Elizabeth's father soon remarried and was so busied with his profession of doctoring there was little time for the vocation of fathering. Her stepmother was faithful to the externals of child raising, but even this lapsed after she bore seven of her own children with Dr. Richard Bayley. And so little Elizabeth Ann Bayley grew up in a world deprived of motherly comforts or fatherly affections.

St. Elizabeth's stepmother, Charlotte Barclay, was diligent in instruction of Holy Scripture. The little girl found the holy writings a great source of inspiration and a refuge from what her own life seemed to lack. Born into the Episcopal faith, Elizabeth found its teachings and guiding precepts strengthened and encouraged her naturally good inclinations. As a young woman she spent much time seeing to the needs of the poor, especially concerned with the plight of the poor and widows. (The association with which Elizabeth Ann Seton had served was the *Society for the Relief of Poor Widows with Small Children.*)

Elizabeth was only a teenager when she met the man she would marry, William Magee Seton, who was already a very accomplished and successful businessman. He was handsome, well traveled, and very much impressed with her loveliness. There was no doubt the feelings were mutual as Elizabeth's diary assures us of that. In 1974 the Rt. Reverend Samuel Provoost, rector of Trinity Church and first bishop of the Protestant Episcopal Diocese of New York, presided at their wedding. Will was 25 and Betty was 19 and both were very much in love.

Married life brought countless joys and blessings to Mrs. Seton. For the first time in her life, there was someone who took the time and pains to love her well. William was a faithful and loving husband, and from their union came five children of their own, Anna Maria, William, Richard, Catherine, and Rebecca.

It was during their later years of married life that the Seton shipping industry began to fail. Financial burdens complicated William's already poor health, and the ruin of the Seton fortunes was imminent. William was advised by doctors to seek a warmer climate for his worsening tubercular condition and to find a way to lessen the monetary pressures he now shouldered.

Elizabeth and William journeyed to Leghorn (Livorno), Italy, in hopes of improving William's health and receiving financial assistance from their shipping partners and good friends, the Filicchis. Only one of their children accompanied them; the oldest, Anna Maria. They could not afford by this time to bring the other four children and consequently left them in the care of relatives. It was

Sr. Mary Hilaire in the room where Mrs. Seton died, inside the White House. She is writing a short Seton biographical story for the *Catholic Sun*, Syracuse and Albany, NY in October of 1975.

an uncomfortable eight-week long trip by sea. William's health grew worse and eight-year-old Anna was sickened by the tossing of the vessel.

Upon arriving in Livorno, the Setons were sentenced to a month in quarantine. It had been rumored that a yellow fever epidemic had broken out in the United States, and William's poor health led Italian officials to believe he might be a carrier. William and his family were locked in a prison cell, which lacked even the barest necessities. It had a dirt floor and bars at the window. The guards had orders to shoot and kill anyone attempting to escape. The ocean spray found its way into the cell, and for 30 days, Elizabeth attended to the needs of her young daughter and her dying husband. Elizabeth wrote a journal during this time, that she might share her experiences with her beloved sister-in-law, Rebecca, back in New York upon their return.

During their stay the Filicchi family did all in their power to alleviate the suffering of their friends during that month. Elizabeth, her husband, and daughter went to nearby Pisa after being freed. There, less than a week later and just after Christmas, William died. Elizabeth had him buried in a Protestant cemetery in Livorno. God had graced the two with nine happy years of married life. In spite of hardships endured, there was greater joy for having shared it all.

Elizabeth's thoughts now turned to her children back home in America. For them she must become both father and mother. Elizabeth anticipated only her return to the states; circumstances, however, did not opportune her departure until four months later.

After William's death Mr. and Mrs. Filicchi insisted Elizabeth and Anna Marie stay with them. It was during her stay in Italy as guests of Antonio and Amabilia Filicchi that she first saw the Catholic faith from a new and enlightening perspective. In Elizabeth's native land, Catholics were primarily from among the poor and pitiful immigrants of Ireland and Germany, people who sold what little they had for passage to a new country in the bowels of human freight ships. More prosperous and much earlier-established Protestants held only contempt for the Catholic people who had done their share of persecuting in Europe and now sought to settle in a land well-founded by mostly Protestant sects.

The inspiring lifestyle of faithful Catholics in Italy at the turn of the 19th century presented Elizabeth with a far more realistic view of the Roman Catholic Church. Elizabeth was most impressed with the daily attendance of mass, not solely reserved for priests, religious and a random few, but a daily mass attended by almost everyone; a church which opened its arms to wealthy and poor alike; a church which joined to honor the Mother of God thrice daily in praying the Angelus; a church which carefully wrapped her soul in penance and prayer as she readied for the celebration of Easter. Indeed, it was a church unlike that which she had distantly perceived in her America. And yet, disfigured by poverty and persecution, it was recognizably the same.

It would be impossible to credit the Filicchis of Livorno with too much kindness. They were the epitome of Christian hospitality with sincere concern for Elizabeth's temporal and spiritual welfare.

It was Elizabeth who initiated her first visit to mass in Italy, but the Filicchis continued to address her interest with education. They taught her the precepts of the Catholic faith and upon returning to New York, Elizabeth, for more than a year, battled intellectually and emotionally the debate of conversion. She could see it would not be pleasant. However, poor "deluded Mrs. Seton," at the expense of family ties and lifelong friendships made her profession of faith in St. Peter's Church on March 14, 1805.

Mrs. Seton, now disowned by her stepmother and disinherited by most of her well-to-do relatives, was faced with the many expenses of raising a family. With no source of income other than that which the Filicchis sent her, Mrs. Seton found employment as a teacher in a private school. (The public school system of education had not yet been established and therefore nearly all schools were privately owned.) Women of high position visited her home and threatened that if she did not quit the education of their sons, fearing she might be teaching them Catholicism, they would remove their sons to another private school and such action would undoubtedly be the ruin of the school which employed her. Mrs. Seton was thus "encouraged" to leave the city of New York.

At the invitation of Archbishop John Carroll (America's first Catholic bishop), Mrs. Seton arrived in Baltimore in 1808. She had expressed her desire to commit herself entirely to Christ. She wanted to become a religious, a woman totally consecrated to the service of God's people.

The Archbishop, very much aware of her vocation as mother, was greatly impressed with her zeal and sanctity, and waived the usual regularities, allowing Mrs. Seton to make vows and to establish a religious community of American sisters, the Sisters of Charity.

It was Mrs. Seton's hope that the Sisters of France, the Daughters of Charity, might come to America to train the infant community in the ways of sisterhood. However, Napoleon prevented such hope and only the Rule of St. Vincent found its way to Baltimore. The rules were somewhat altered and approved for their use in the United States.

Unanimously chosen as head of the community, Mrs. Seton was now referred to as Mother Seton. Members of her little band likewise donned the widow garb Mrs. Seton had worn since the death of her husband in Italy. Archbishop John Carroll invested the group in the basement chapel of St. Mary's Church in Baltimore.

Mother Seton remained in Baltimore for only a year. The community of five, her daughters and two sisters-in-law journeyed to Emmitsburg, Maryland, where

Mother Seton and her little group established the cradle of Catholic education in the United States.

They first lived in a log cabin at Mount St. Mary's, then six weeks later moved into the Flemming Farmhouse, often referred to as the Stone House. When Archbishop Carroll came to visit, he found the community had grown and the stone farmhouse held 16 people within its two-room (plus attic) structure. He insisted better accommodations be made. A much larger, more adequate home was constructed. It was called the White House, and there are those who consider this to be the site of America's first Catholic school. It was the house in which Mother Seton died.

Before her death Mother Seton lived to see her community grow to 50 members. She also saw her Emmitsburg school grow and succeed. She sent her sisters to begin America's first Catholic orphanage in Philadelphia, and others to New York City to establish a second orphanage there. After her death her community established the first American Catholic hospital in St. Louis. Also following her death, Emmitsburg and the St. Louis Sisters of Charity joined with the Vincentian Daughters of Charity in France.

Currently, the correct name of the community at Emmitsburg is Daughters of Charity of Saint Vincent de Paul, not "Sisters of Charity", (since 1850). Meanwhile other branches of Mother Seton's community in New York City, Cincinnati, OH, Halifax, Nova Scotia, Convent Station, NJ and Greensburg, PA, have preferred to remain independent American communities, and refer to themselves as "Sisters of Charity".

[Please forgive my utter digression, but I was a Sister of St. Francis of Syracuse, NY and our Sisters in Hawaii were often referred to as the "Sisters of Charity" simply because of what they did. These women worked with the sick and the lepers, and the people of Hawaii did not think of us as "Franciscan" as much as they thought we were just "sisters of charity"!]

Both of Mother Seton's sons, William and Richard Seton, graduated from Mt. St. Mary's Seminary at Emmitsburg and served in the US Navy. They also spent some time working for the Filicchis in Italy. To the embarrassment of their mother, neither son repaid in any way the years of Filicchi generosity.

Once having left the "Emmitsburg nest," neither William nor Richard showed much interest in the concerns of their mother. Most letters contained requests for money. Mother Seton had taken a vow of poverty, but not her sons. In order to get the money they needed, she would often write and beg of friends, if necessary.

Neither William nor Richard was present at her death. William was the only Seton child to marry and bear children; however, there are no living direct descendants. Richard died at the age of 24 after nursing a clergyman with scarlet fever. The clergyman survived, but Richard contracted the fever, died and was buried at sea only two years after of death of Mother Seton in 1821.

Mrs. Seton had three daughters. The oldest, Anna Maria (nicknamed Annina) entered the Sisters of Charity at 16 but died less than a year later of tuberculosis. Only four years later, Mother Seton's youngest child, Rebecca, died at 14 as the result of a skating accident. With an infected hip, Rebecca could not sit, stand or lie in any position without great suffering. Frequently Mother Seton would spend her nights holding her daughter so that Bec might find some rest her in arms.

The last surviving daughter, Catherine, was the only child present at Mother Seton's deathbed. Almost 10 years after her mother's death, Catherine went to New York City to become a Sister of Mercy. She later became their Mother General, and died at the age of 90, although into her 91st year.

Shortly before Mother Seton died, she asked to be brought downstairs so that she might be next to chapel and spend her dying moments close to the Blessed Sacrament. A plaque which marks her place of death reads: "Here near this door by this fireplace on an old and lowly couch, died our cherished and saintly Mother Seton on the 4th of January, 1821. She died in poverty, but rich in faith and good works. May we, her children, walk in her footsteps and share one day in her happiness. Amen."

Among her dying words were: "Be children of the church!" "Blood of Jesus, wash me." "May the most just, the most high, and the most amiable will of God be accomplished forever." Mrs. Seton was sixteen years a Catholic, thirty-one years a Protestant and all of her life a faithful follower and servant of Christ. May we never forget the love of this valiant life, lived in faith, hope, and charity.

Promoting Mother Seton. My sister Michele, myself, my mother Catherine, and brother Chris. Taken in our Lorain home by the *Cleveland Catholic Bulletin*, in January, 1976.

CHAPTER SIX

After the Canonization

When I returned from Rome, Kathleen Hessert from a Syracuse television station called to interview me. Mother Viola gave me permission, and it was a joy to talk about my dear friend, Mother Seton. By now I knew a good deal about her life and frequently gave talks to local parish groups. Almost every year I led a bus filled with pilgrims to Emmitsburg, Maryland, and routinely gave the groups a three-hour long talk on the public address system during the trip.

I planned a diocesan celebration with Bishop Foery of Syracuse and the various Catholic schools. It was a wonderful way to mark the first year of Mother Seton's feast day after her canonization.

I stayed in touch with my Albany New York Daughter of Charity friend, Sr. Sylvia Borden. She was one of three Daughters approximately my age who has befriended me over the years.

Sr. Mary Ruth Morrow, the Daughter who introduced me to Mother Seton in Washington, DC, left her community and later married Edward Smith. When I did try to communicate with Mary Ruth, she still would not tell me why she had decided to distance herself. I wouldn't learn why until after I left my community in 1984.

Ann O'Neill and I did not waste any time getting in touch once we were back in the states. I invited Ann to spend a weekend with me at Holy Trinity in Syracuse. I was so excited when she decided to leave her husband and four children for a few days to take time for us to get to know each other.

We talked incessantly and it was great fun for us both. We went to confession at Assumption Church, my first parish assignment, and Ann mused that I received a larger penance from the priest than she did. I told her that nuns are not at all free from making poor choices. Over the following years I would be invited to Ann's home to meet her sisters and get to know her mother.

Top: Sr. Mary Hilaire and Ann O'Neill Hooe. Taken at the Syracuse, NY Motherhouse, 1975.

Bottom: Sr. Mary Hilaire Tavenner and Ann O'Neill Hooe with her four children: Joseph, Robert (now deceased), Mary Alice and Gerard. Taken October, 1977 in the Emmitsburg community cemetery.

In fact, more often than not, when I took a bus trip of pilgrims to Emmitsburg, Ann and her mother, Mrs. Felixena O'Neill, would stay with us at the Rambler Motel in Thurmont, MD. The pilgrims loved meeting Ann, and I loved sharing a weekend with her. When I was transferred to Lorain, Ohio in 1978 to teach in my home parish, my mother would join the annual bus trip, and Ann's mother and my mother became good friends.

During most of those pilgrimages, Rev. Fr. Sylvester Taggart, C.M. the Vice Postulator for the cause for canonization of Mother Seton, would preside at the Elizabeth Ann Seton Shrine mass for the groups. Fr. Taggart was a remarkably gentle and soft-spoken man. I consider him one of the most humble priests I have ever known. Often when I gave a talk on Mother Seton, I would be given $5.00 or $10.00 as a thank you. I sent the money to the Mother Seton Guild. Fr. Taggart was the director, and he would send me another batch of Mother Seton holy cards for me to distribute after future talks.

During visits to the shrine store, I would purchase relics of Mother Seton and give them away. These relics are no longer available, as there were only a certain amount of her bones made available to the public. When my nephew, Garth Montgomery Tavenner, died, I donated such a relic to Elizabeth Ann Seton Church in Edgewood, near Moriarity, New Mexico, where my brother's family lived. The New Mexico branch of our family worshipped/worships in Our Lady of Mt. Carmel Parish in Moriarity, but currently there is talk of these two parishes merging.

Also, there was a woman by the name of Elizabeth Ann Garrett Schermerhorn from Fulton, New York, to whom I had given a relic. I taught two of her three children and was very impressed with her and her family. Betty Schermerhorn shared Elizabeth Ann Seton's first and middle name, and when she was diagnosed with cancer, I believed with all my heart that perhaps 51 year-old Betty might receive a miracle.

After three years of treatments, it became evident this would not happen. Her husband, Walt, was understandably angry that the prayers to Mother Seton, the relic, and all the hope in the world could not spare Betty's life. What she did receive was a very holy death, surrounded by husband, her son, two daughters, Fr. Joseph Champlin, her parish priest, and three friends.

From this side we cannot see or understand the true impact of our faith and our prayers. What I do know is that Betty died in January of 1976, but the memory of her strong faith, devotion to family and her church lives strong in those of us who came to know her, and have not forgotten.

I have also given a relic to my home parish, St. Anthony of Padua in Lorain, OH, but it is impossible for me to recall all the relics I have purchased and given away over the years. During those years after Mother Seton's canonization, I was ever so fervent in spreading devotion to her.

The year following Mother Seton's canonization I was advised by the education director in our community, Sr. Eloise Emm, that I would be matriculating at St. Charles Seminary in Philadelphia. I wanted to earn a master's degree in theology and had written a letter of inquiry to Fr. Joseph Dirvin, who was working at St. John's College in Jamaica, New York. Fr. Dirvin was the priest who had written that first Seton biography that Sr. Mary Ruth had given me in Washington, D.C. When Father wrote back to me he explained he could not teach me in class as he was working in administration at the time. He was willing to meet with me on occasion, but I wanted more time than that, so I didn't pursue that direction.

Sr. Eloise arranged that three of our community would matriculate at St. Charles Seminary in Philadelphia during our summers. What I found interesting was that Sr. Marita Edward, the nun I met along with Sr. Elizabeth Seton in New York City while en route to the Canonization the year before, was also a student at the seminary. Small world.

It was during my summers at the St. Charles that I got to know Sr. Marita Edward and learned of her miraculous cure from cancer. Her older friend, Sr. Elizabeth Seton would visit campus, and I got to know her better too. At first Sr. Marita and I hit it off pretty well, but our relationship cooled after I upset her. I gave her an opinion she really didn't ask for or seem interested in having. When I look back at my words, I think I might have been wiser to say nothing. She's a delightful and dynamic woman, but we no longer have contact. She left her community in the late 1980's or early 1990's, I believe. Not everyone we come to know in this life as "friend" can possibly stay in our lives. There is not "time" or "room" enough for all the holy people we come to know and love to "literally" stay, because we all have special work to accomplish. I think that is why some are in our lives only temporarily. The memory of the love is what most of us carry forth. In Heaven, it is possible, however, to love and still be with all our sacred relationships at the same time! In God, (and with God) all things are possible!

During my second summer at St. Charles Seminary I met a Daughter of Charity, Sr. Frances Anne Odum. We both played guitars and would do folk masses together and eventually struck up a very pleasant friendship. What I especially enjoyed was her directness. She was very honest with me, and at times, I found it difficult to befriend some of Mother Seton's spiritual daughters.

Frances Anne could see the best in me. She is the third of the three Daughters who became friends. First, Sr. Mary Ruth Morrill Smith in Washington, then Sr. Sylvia Borden in Albany, New York, and now Sr. Frances Anne at the seminary in Philadelphia. All three of them have left their community over the years but all three were very dynamic religious women.

While in Philadelphia during the summers of 1976 until 1982, I had the opportunity to do some research on Elizabeth Ann Seton's best friend, Juliana Sitgreaves Scott. I was the first pilgrim to Juliana's grave in Philadelphia and was able to find and visit with her living descendants. I shared this information with the Emmitsburg Provincial House Archives. On January 4, 1979, the Philadelphia Catholic Standard and Times published a story I had written for Philadelphia about Julia Scott, and I will reprint that story in the next chapter. Don't you think it interesting that the patron saint of Livorno, Italy, where Mrs. Seton received the seeds of conversion, is St. Julia?

CHAPTER SEVEN

Elizabeth's Philadelphia Friend

Seldom have the pages of history left such heart-warming testimony of a more loving relationship than that of St. Elizabeth Ann Seton and Mrs. Juliana Sitgreaves Scott. We're not exactly sure how they met, but 17-year old Betsy Bayley, the future St. Elizabeth, did not live very far from 26-year old Mrs. Scott when she and her husband resided on Broadway in New York City. Mrs. Scott's husband was a famed lawyer. Betsy's father was a prominent New York City physician, and the two young women enjoyed a very comfortable and prestigious social circle.

Horseback riding near the East River, talking together, and many other simple pleasures became the unobtrusive beginnings of a profound and lasting friendship. Of the many and solid relationships Elizabeth Ann Bayley enjoyed throughout her life (Archbishop John Carroll, Alexander Hamilton, Antonio Filicchi, George Washington, Bishop Brute, and Bishop John Dubois, to name but a few), the one with Juliana Sitgreaves Scott was uncontestedly the most cherished.

Juliana (also called Julia) Scott was the granddaughter of Sarah and William Sitgreaves, both of England. They immigrated to America in 1729, only a year after their marriage, and settled in Philadelphia. Their second child, William, born in Philadelphia, married Susannah Deshon in Boston in 1756. William and Susannah were Juliana's father and mother. Both of her parents are buried in Christ Church Cemetery.

Juliana was the oldest daughter and fifth child of William and Susannah Sitgreaves. She was born on May 15, 1765 and baptized on November 7th at Christ Church of Philadelphia. Juliana married Lewis Allaire Scott on January 18, 1785, probably in the Sitgreaves home. Soon after their marriage, Julia and Lewis moved to New York where the treasured friendship of Betsy and Julia began.

After 13 years of marriage, Lewis died at the early age of 39. By this time young Betsy Bayley had become Mrs. William Magee Seton and, having already shared several years of friendship with Julia, never left her side day or night during the excess of her sorrows. Elizabeth helped Julia to pack and close her house in preparation for her return to Philadelphia. Having suffered the loss of her husband, Julia decided to take her son, John Morin, and her daughter, Maria, home to the security of her own family.

Five years after Julia had been widowed, Elizabeth's own husband, William Magee Seton, died in Pisa, Italy. Elizabeth and William had traveled to Italy to secure financial assistance from the Filicchi family and also had hoped the Mediterranean climate would improve William's tubercular condition. It was here, while in Livorno, that Mrs. Seton began to understand and accept the teachings of the Catholic church. Up until this time she had been a devout Episcopalian. (Her mother's father had been the rector of St. Andrew's Parish on Staten Island.)

Elizabeth's conversion did not take place until almost a year and a half after her return to New York City. Mrs. Seton, socialite and highly esteemed member of the "upper echelon," now became an object of ridicule by both family and friends. No one could understand her desire to leave the Episcopal faith for Catholicism.

By this time, with the death of her husband and the complete collapse of his shipping firm, Mrs. Seton experienced severe financial ruin as well. Even well-to-do family members refused to assist her in the rearing of her five children. Now she became dependent upon the charity and unlimited generosity of basically two friends: Antonio Filicchi of Livorno, Italy and Juliana Sitgreaves Scott, daughter of Philadelphia and life-long friend to her.

Julia and Elizabeth had enjoyed nearly 13 years of friendship together in New York City before Julia's return home to Philadelphia. For 22 years after that they continued to exchange letters. A most extraordinary book containing most of Elizabeth's letters to "her Glorianna" is entitled *Letters of Mother Seton to Mrs. Scott*. Joseph Code edited the book copyrighted in 1929, and the original letters are now in the protected custody of the Sisters of Charity, Emmitsburg, Maryland.

The following are a few brief excerpts taken from the letters Mrs. Seton wrote to Julia Scott. During 1798, Elizabeth wrote: "My thoughts turn to you, dear Julia, with whom I have so often shared the cheerfulness of the blazing fire, and the feeling tones of my sweet piano. Oh, Julia, Julia, never again! Those hours are past, which though I enjoyed them, I never knew their value!"

In 1803, the day before Elizabeth set sail for Italy, she wrote, "And in this sacred hour my soul implores for you, the friend of my first and warmest affections, that peace which God alone can give."

In 1813, with poetry and passion, Elizabeth says to her friend, "My children, Julia, must fight it out as their mother did before them, looking to Providence and beyond the grave. But if they do not I hope they will be punished by

The Stone House, first convent in the valley, as it was being moved from its original location to its current site, across from the Provincial House in the fall of 1979. Photo by MHT.

disappointments and adversity until they do. What a hard-hearted mother! Yes, you dear little Glorianna, if you yourself could be made to see with the eyes of your soul and pierce these clouds of mortal cares which conceal from you the perspective of Eternity, I would be glad to see you too . . . dare I say it? Yes. To see you under the iron hand which would conduct you to His feet, to the feet of your Father, who when you acknowledge his claims, would hold you near Him by silken cords, until in true and filial love you would desire to leave Him never."

In 1820, several months before her death, Elizabeth says to her friend, "Oh, may our God bless you is the heartful prayer of your E. A. Seton."

After Elizabeth's conversion there were many family pressures. Julia wrote to Elizabeth and offered to adopt her oldest daughter, Anna Maria, at two different times, hoping it might relieve some of the burden of her financial situation. Elizabeth greatly appreciated the gesture but could not bear to part with any of her children.

By 1814, Elizabeth Seton had already founded the Sisters of Charity among the Blue Ridge Mountains of Emmitsburg, MD. During this year Mother Seton's youngest daughter, Rebecca, was suffering a severe hip injury from a winter fall. Julia paid the cost of the most excellent doctors available. Rebecca went to Philadelphia for medical attention, where Julia doted upon the girl and attended to her every need.

In the fall of 1814, Mother Seton sent three of her religious congregation, the Sisters of Charity, to manage St. Joseph's Orphanage in Philadelphia. This was the first official branching of the Emmitsburg settlement, and became the first Catholic orphanage in the United States. Even here the generous hand of Julia Sitgreaves Scott was felt and deeply appreciated.

In the spring of 1815, Mother Seton had decided to entrust her older son, William, who had recently graduated from Mt. St. Mary's of Emmitsburg, to the Filicchi family in Italy, where he might acquire a knowledge of business and later obtain a good position. Mother Seton was able to meet the expense of the journey with the money sent her by Mrs. Scott.

In the spring of 1818, Elizabeth sent her daughter, Catherine, to visit "Aunt" Julia to improve her poor health. Catherine Josephine Seton was the fourth child of Elizabeth and William Seton. She was also Julia Scott's god-daughter. After Mother Seton died in 1821 Julia provided a very handsome $1,000.00 inheritance for Catherine, if she had not married by the time of Julia's death.

It seems evident that Catherine did receive this money, because when Julia died in 1842 Catherine was unmarried. Only four years after this, Catherine became the first American postulant to enter the Sisters of Mercy at Dobbs Ferry, NY. She brought with her $1,000 upon entering and gave another $1,000 upon profession. Some of this money may have been earned from the teaching Catherine had done before becoming a nun, bur very likely some may have come from one of the greatest benefactors Elizabeth Seton and her Sisters of Charity had ever known, Philadelphia's Julia. Sister Catherine Seton later became the Mother General of the Community at Dobbs Ferry, and died at the ripe old age of 90 plus.

The debt that American Catholics owe to this generous member of Philadelphia's fashionable society is beyond computation. But the loving relationship Eliza and Julia shared was by no means one-sided! It was very true that Julia repeatedly supported Mother Seton and her endeavors with her own personal fortune, but Elizabeth had likewise borne the sorrows and spiritual trials Julia had known. They carried each other.

Julia's much-loved brother, John Sitgreaves, died unmarried of yellow fever in Germantown at the age of 35 (and is buried in the German Baptist Congregation Graveyard.) Only two years later Julia buried her father. She then convinced her mother to come and live with her, and eight years later Julia's mother also died. Julia's son, John Morin Scott, was the mayor of Philadelphia during a time referred to as "the-know-nothing riots," a period of civil and religious unrest.

Actually there are many other strong ties between the city of Philadelphia and America's first native-born saint, but none so touching or so vibrant as the loving friendship of Mrs. Scott and Mrs. Seton.

CHAPTER EIGHT

A Time for Miracles

Back in the 1970's the rules to get a foundress canonized required two miracles to precede an exhumation of the body. Then beatification could take place if the Congregation for the Causes of Saints in Rome approved. Beatification permits the individual to be honored and recognized as being in heaven but the individual is only promulgated in his or her respective country. Holy cards, relics, intercessory prayers, etc. are distributed within the country of origin, but with canonization the individual is honored throughout the Catholic world. Canonization could not happen for Mrs. Seton, according to the rules, unless two more miracles happened after her beatification.

When I say miracles I don't use this word lightly. There have to be legal, well-documented, intensive studies into the "miracle". The Devil's Advocate will try to prove, in every manner, that the event was merely a fortunate circumstance of luck, chance, or coincidence. The job of the Devil's Advocate is to explain the "miracle" away. The proof may take years of research to collect, then it must be presented via tribunals established for the cause.

In the case of Mother Seton, one of her spiritual daughters, Sr. Gertrude Korzendorfer, was cured of pancreatic cancer in 1935, and Ann Teresa O'Neill Hooe was cured of acute lymphatic leukemia in 1952. This opened the door for the exhumation of Mother Seton's body. On March 17, 1963, Blessed Elizabeth Ann Seton was beatified in Rome. But now Rome required two more miracles for a canonization.

A third miracle took place in 1963. Carl Eric Kalin, a Lutheran who suffered from the combination of red measles and inflammation of the brain, became comatose. This generally results in either death or severe brain damage. For

Mr. Kalin, after his Catholic wife placed a relic of Mother Seton upon him, praying, Carl awoke and resumed a perfectly normal life. But there was no fourth miracle.

Only a few months before Mother Seton's canonization was announced Archbishop William Borders, the Archbishop of Baltimore, flew to Rome to meet with Paul VI to successfully persuade the Pope to dispense with the need for a second (the fourth) confirmed miracle. Because the other three miracles were so well-documented, Archbishop Borders reported that the Holy Father was easily persuaded to forgo this demanding Vatican standard.

Speaking of miracles, some considered the waiver of a fourth to be a miracle in itself. Then, the talk of a Hollywood movie about the life of Mother Seton was considered by others to be a fourth. Yes, ABC was planning to produce a $3 million dollar movie for television about the life of a saint!

I first learned of the news one day after teaching school in Lorain in December of 1979. I had lain down for a short rest after teaching and was called to the phone. It was a producer from MGM studios in Hollywood. Beverlee Dean explained to me that they wanted to make a docudrama on the life of St. Elizabeth Ann Seton.

She told me the script was almost finished and asked if I would read it and look for mistakes. "Ann O'Neill Hooe told us about you," she explained. This news was almost as exciting as the day I learned Mother Seton would be canonized! I could hardly believe my ears. I told her, "Yes, send the script. I'll read it and let you know whatever changes I might suggest." I'm quite sure many others were asked to do this as well.

Then I called Ann to thank her. I was happy to help without any thought of payment. After that, Beverlee would call to give me updates as to how well the process was going. Originally the plan was to air the program for Mother's Day of 1980 but later it was decided to wait until the Christmas season of 1980, to show the film. At first the movie was called "Mother Seton", but later the title was changed to "A Time for Miracles."

Beverlee called to say they didn't have a leading lady for the part of Mother Seton as of yet, and asked me to keep this in prayer. So I asked my students to pray for a great leading lady. There were several suggested names; I only recall Marlo Thomas, Danny Thomas's daughter. Then later I was told they had chosen Kate Mulgrew.

I was thrilled. The decision was last minute as filming took place in January and February of 1980. In time, Beverlee invited me on location so that I could meet Kate and help the cast with getting to know more about the life and character of Mrs. Seton. Ann O'Neill Hooe was also invited, but she and her husband were having some marital issues and she thought it better not to attend.

Top: Shrine Altar of **Blessed** Elizabeth Seton. Note: Bronze and silver casket containing her relics. Photo taken circa 1974.

Bottom: Shrine Altar of **Saint** Elizabeth Seton. Note: Casket with relics was interred beneath the altar after the Canonization, and is no longer visible.

When I asked my Mother General to go to Georgia for a weekend, she asked me, "Sister, if Mother Seton has 7,000 spiritual daughters, how is it that they want a Franciscan Sister to advise them on this film?" I couldn't answer exactly as I knew the film crew was in touch with Fr. Dirvin, Emmitsburg, and other important Mother Seton contacts. I explained that it was Ann Hooe who had suggested I help.

My boss (the Mother General) wasn't really happy about these circumstances, but reluctantly gave me permission to go to Georgia. They would not be filming in Emmitsburg, Maryland, as it was winter, and Georgia was south enough that they could create winter weather scenes if necessary. Sr. Aileen, our Mother General, told me I could not do anything in public but that I could help. So when they asked me to be in the film and asked me to do a talk show to help promote the project while we were filming, I had to tell them no. I didn't mind. I was just so happy this was all actually happening.

My mother drove me to the airport. And what was supposed to be a weekend became a ten-day long visit. I got to know the cast and crew pretty well during that time. I became very attached to many of them, especially Kate.

One particular morning when I came on location, Beverlee snatched me quickly to say Jimmy Carter's mother-in-law was there. Miss Allie Smith had come to watch the filming with some of her best friends: Miss Polly Peters, Miss Mary and Miss Elizabeth. I was assigned the task of explaining what scene was taking place, then took them on tour of the mess hall, the make-up trailer, and wardrobe. They were having a great visit. So much so they invited Beverlee, an extra named Theresa Filibert, and me to go with them to Plains, Ga. They wanted to return the hospitality and this was just as much fun for us. We all traveled in their van and they gave us the grand tour.

We went to Jimmy and Rosalynn's house (they were living in the White House at the time), past the security guards, so that we could walk onto the porch and about the yard, then to Miss Allie's home, down Main Street, over to the train station, etc. I sat next to Rosalynn's mother in the van and we both enjoyed each other's company. Several years later when I was sent to teach in Florida, I was able to visit Miss Allie and our friendship and visits continued long after I left the community. For almost 20 years Ms. Alethea (Allie) Smith became a kind of surrogate grandmother. I spent weekends with her in Plains and she took me everywhere.

The first time I met Rosalynn was in her mother's home. I had arrived for a weekend visit and Miss Allie called her daughter to come over to meet me. That was pretty humbling. Rosalynn had been to visit my hometown of Lorain and recalled two things about being here: the magnificent crystal candelabra in our Palace Theatre and the warmth of the people in our community.

Getting to know Miss Allie also gave me to the opportunity to meet President Jimmy Carter several times, and get to know Rosalynn better as well as her siblings Murray (now deceased) and Allethea, Rosalynn's sister.

That encounter I made with Miss Allie during the time of filming the Mother Seton movie lasted for the next twenty years, until she died on April 1st of 2000 at the age of 95. We shared many letters, phone calls and visits. I could write a book about our many adventures together. She reminded me of my mother's mother, gentle, sweet, sincere, and gracious.

The time I spent with Kate, Beverlee, and all the others was incredibly memorable, but I won't write too many of the details just now as I have included many of them in the next chapter. Upon returning from Georgia, I began the work of promoting the film to everyone I knew or thought might care. I was glad they had changed the airing date to Christmastime of 1980 because it gave me more time to spread the word. When the movie did air the ratings were low because so few Americans tuned in to watch it.

For the next three years Kate Mulgrew and I became the best of friends. She came to meet my mother in Lorain and stayed at the convent with me. Kate flew me to New York for her birthday party and we met in Syracuse several times. She flew me to her wedding in Dubuque, Iowa, where I got to meet and know her parents and family. It was a whirlwind friendship, but it all ended when I left the community.

Her mother explained to me on the phone one Christmas Eve about five years after I left the convent, "Well, Hilaire, you're not a sister anymore. Things just aren't the same."

Kate never personally explained her departure from my life to me, and though I found it painful, I also understand a person's freedom to be in or not be in relationship. Ironically in 1999 Kate married a man by the name of Tim Hagan, a commissioner for Cuyahoga County, (Cleveland, Ohio area) and when Mr. Hagan ran for governor of Ohio, Kate visited the Lorain area to help his campaign. Kate knew I lived here but she didn't choose to be in touch. Sometimes people are only meant to be in our lives for a while, not forever.

Before the movie was to air I wrote a story for a newspaper editor in Syracuse, New York. I had written a story for Sam Vacarro at the *Syracuse Herald-American* before and somehow he had learned of my being involved with the Mother Seton movie. (I probably told him!) Anyway, Sam asked me to write a story for their weekly newsmagazine about my adventure, and I did. I had to receive permission from our Mother General as nothing could ever be published without permission. At first she said, "Yes."

Then I received a call from Sam, telling me that the Mother General had contacted him and didn't want the story to run. He liked the story so much and really wanted to see it published, so he told Sr. Aileen, "I'm sorry, but it's too late. The story is already in process and I can't stop it now." He confided to me that he hadn't actually told her the truth, and asked if I would be upset if he ran it. I told him, "Go ahead." I felt the publicity would help to bring in more viewers. The

Mother General before Sr. Aileen, Mother Viola, had always been supportive of my work for Mother Seton, so this was difficult for me to understand.

The next chapter of this book will be the story that was published on December 7th, 1980 in the *Syracuse Herald-American*. Though I have deleted parts of the article, I apologize for some parts which are repetitive, though essential for continuity.

CHAPTER NINE

Nun Sees TV Stars Acting Like Saints

I had just come home from school, thoroughly exhausted. I was half-aware of the phone ringing. A woman asked for me. "This is Beverlee Dean and I'm calling from MGM Studios in Hollywood, California. We are planning to make a film on the life of Elizabeth Ann Seton, and Ann Hooe said you might be willing to help us."

At the time I never could have imagined how much this one phone call on December 5, 1979, would affect my life. It would bring me into the midst of movie stars, the state of Georgia, and countless memorable, incredible circumstances.

I was teaching science to sixth, seventh, and eight graders in Lorain, Ohio. I'd been a teacher for 12 years and a Sister of St. Francis, Syracuse, for the last 14. The routine for school sisters is fairly common. Getting involved with a national ABC Circle Theatre Presentation is an exciting and new ball game.

"Beverlee, will you please say that again. I don't think I understand."

Beverlee explained she was a co-producer of an ABC film on Mother Seton. It's scheduled to be aired on December 21st, 1980, as a Christmas special. She had called Ann Hooe in Maryland to discuss the movie. Ann had received a documented miracle which brought about the Beatification of Mrs. Seton on March 17, 1963.

Beverlee said Ann told her, "If you really want to talk to someone who knows about Mother Seton and loves her you should call my friend, Sr. Mary Hilaire."

Beverlee asked for my prayers and said she wanted the film to be absolutely accurate and well-done. I promised to pray. Then she asked if I would read Henry Denker's script. A Jewish author with many state and television credits,

---

68

Denker spent 10 years writing, directing, and producing "The Greatest Story Ever Told" for film.

Two days later I received the script with a note to edit, add, comment, do anything I thought might help, and send it back as soon as possible. Within 48 hours it was on its way back to Beverlee.

It wasn't a difficult job but more of a pleasure. I believed the script was good, about 75% accurate. Not bad for Hollywood. I corrected the obvious mistakes like names, dates, children out of order, etc.

I was pleased, later, to see so many of the changes made in the finished script but had to accept license for editing and adapting to film and the fact of so much limited time. The only real flaw I was aware of (without yet having seen the finished product) is how much of the story remains untold. A three-hour film cannot do justice to 46 ½ intense, inspired and courageous years of life.

Beverlee was grateful for my help. She called frequently, keeping me informed as they prepared for filming. Michael O'Herlihy was signed as director. (One of his projects was directing "Backstairs at the White House.) The pressure was on when no leading lady was cast and filming was less than a month away. Many women were turned down or refused the part.

Only two weeks before filming, Beverlee called to tell me Kate Mulgrew (of "Mrs. Columbo," "Kate Loves a Mystery," and the original Mary Ryan of "Ryan's Hope") had been signed to play Mother Seton. I wondered if this was typical casting procedure for a $2.7 million film.

I thought of Kate's signing as more than anything an answer to prayer, even though I never had seen her on television and hardly could visualize her.

A month later I received a call from Kate Mulgrew. I was in the midst of preparing supper for the seven of us missioned in St. Anthony's Convent. When she introduced herself I felt a surge of excitement, almost disbelief. I had never spoken to a movie star. It was a real lift, especially after peeling potatoes, seasoning the chicken, and fidgeting with the salad.

Her voice was firm, full, and articulate.

I may have stammered.

She said she needed my help. Would I please send her some information or books that would help her to better understand the character of the woman she portrayed? Although Kate had known of Mother Seton since childhood, she wanted her role to be as authentic as possible.

Within 10 minutes after our conversation, I had packaged three of my favorite books and various articles and was en route to the local post office. First class next-day delivery to Savannah, GA. And still home in time to put the supper on the table.

On February 8, two days later, Beverlee was on the phone. "Sister, you really must come to Georgia. We need to meet you; you should be a part of this." She had mentioned this before, but I wondered, would it really happen? As a teacher, I knew if it did, it could only be for a weekend.

First I'd need to talk with my superior, Sr. William Clare Ryan. She remarked, "Call that producer back and tell her protocol is to invite the superior as well." Sister Nancy Emerick, another sister living with us, piped in, "Hilaire, you can't go without a secretary. I'll be your secretary!" I had all kinds of offers but Beverlee was sending only one plane ticket.

St. Aileen Griffin, our Superior General, didn't mind my visiting the filming location but questioned my participation. Why me, a Franciscan? Why not a Sister of Charity, one of Mother Seton's own spiritual daughters?

I didn't understand either.

I called my mother who lived only a block from our convent. Mom was excited for me; what an intriguing prospect! My enthusiasm could not waver. I believed in Beverlee, in Kate, and the excellent script I had read. They had filmed in Savannah for two weeks and would now be in Columbus, GA for two weeks.

It was settled. I was to fly from Cleveland Friday after school on February 15th. I would arrive in Atlanta in time for a puddle jumper to Columbus. I'm not especially fond of flying, "Nearer my God to Thee" and all, but this particular flight was more about, how is this all possible?

Beverlee was in Columbus to meet me. I never pictured her short, stocky, blond or Italian, but she was. She was also delightfully sincere in every conversation we shared. Beverlee and I talked that night until 3 AM. The next morning we went directly to the set, almost 30 miles from our Holiday Inn, to an historic settlement called Westville, built around 1850, not far from (would you believe?) Lumpkin, Georgia.

We arrived to find 100 to 150 people at "New York City's historic St. Peter's Church". Some were extras in the film, others spectators; many were cast and crew. Out of the church came running a little figure of a woman dressed in an early 1800 Italian widow's garb, black bonnet and all. It was Kate. She embraced me with the most warm and sincere greeting I ever received from a person I had never met. This first image of Kate will remain indelible.

She was beautiful and much younger than I expected. I was 32; I thought she would be at least 35. She was 24.

The first scene I watched being filmed was Mrs. Seton (by then a widow and mother of five children) receiving her First Holy Communion. Four or five other scenes were filmed that day; I thoroughly enjoyed them all, intensely watching Kate with a critical eye, searching to discover a semblance of Mother Seton. Yes, I sensed her. Kate moved and spoke with a strength, a warmth, a presence. This was not a sensational or distorted performance, but an authentic and conceivable presentation of the saint I love. That evening Kate and I had dinner in her trailer. We talked about everything. I imagine she may have been as curious about a nun as I was about a movie star. I believed she was perfect for the part.

Top: Sr. Mary Hilaire and Kate Mulgrew as Mrs. Seton.

Bottom: Sr. Mary Hilaire and Kate Mulgrew as Mother Seton.

Taken during the filming of "A Time for Miracles" in February of 1980.

We went out to watch the late-hour filming. The director was creating a mob scene, a rather violent moment of tension where Catholic and Protestant bigotry collide in front of St. Peter's Church, New York City.

Mrs. Seton had been a prominent Episcopalian of Trinity Episcopal Church there, and her conversion to the Catholic faith added to the religious animosities.

O'Herlihy kept the cast and crew working that night until 1:30 AM. It turned very cold and costumes were not much comfort. The mob became more and more angry, take after take. I think a few of that gang would have liked to attack the director.

My first full day was the most memorable. Meeting Fr. Joseph Dirvin, author of *Mrs. Seton,* the book upon which the movie was based, was a very special honor. His was the first book I ever read about Elizabeth Seton. It made a profound impression.

Sunday morning Kate and I attended mass in Fr. Dirvin's hotel room along with Jimmy Hawkins, Beverlee's co-producer, and Theresa Filbert, an extra in the cast and a good friend of Beverlee's. Bev couldn't make it because of a serious ear infection.

After mass Kate and I went to one of the more elegant restaurants in Columbus. People recognized her and it wasn't easy for us to talk with constant interruptions. They wanted her autograph or an exchange of words. I sincerely felt sorry for her and began to realize how precious my private life really is.

Several hours later we went back to the Holiday Inn. I set up my slide projector in Kate's room and spent the next two hours explaining to Kate and Hoolihan Burke (who played Sr. Maria Murphy, one of Mother Seton's very first postulants) about Mother Seton, the shrine in Emmitsburg, MD, and the canonization ceremony in Rome.

After my presentation the three of us went for coffee in the dining room. I joked with them. "We ought to have a reunion in Lorain! The two of you should come to our convent for a weekend sometime."

Kate laughed and added a wry, amusing reply, "Yes, Hilaire, but what will the sisters say when I arrive with 14 trunks? Or when I send my steak back to the kitchen because it's too rare? Or when you have to leave your students to get me a cold drink?" We had lots of good laughs; I liked them both very much.

That evening I showed my slide collection to Beverlee, Nan Mason (Sr. Rose White in the film), Allison Biggers, (Sr. Mary Ann Butler) and Theresa Filibert.

In the middle of my explanations Beverlee blurted, "Sister, how can you leave us? Your students, your school, your parish, your family have you every day—can't you possibly stay with us for the rest of the week? I will gladly pay for your substitute! There is only one more week of filming. Your being here means so much to us."

(Could she possibly know how much it meant to me?) I must admit I was torn. I hated to ask so much of my sisters in Lorain. I knew their workload already was straining.

I called Sr. Rose Alice Carberry, my principal. She was more than kind. She didn't hesitate to tell me she would take my students and everything would be covered. I should stay for the rest of the week. Sister believed this project needed me.

That week reminded me so much of the week I spent in Rome for the canonization back in 1975. There were so many parallels—the most significant, a feeling Saint Elizabeth Ann Seton was there with me approving of this remarkable endeavor and these very fine people.

I spent the rest of the week with Kate, the cast and crew, discovering them and becoming what each of us felt we needed to be, singing, concentrating, praying, reflecting, discussing.

I was surprised to find them so much like other people I have known. I learned of marital, health and personal problems. They were so honest and forthright that I felt very comfortable. The only vulgarities I heard all week were a few choice words a man in transportation voiced after backing his van into a pole.

One evening at supper I told Kate how amazed I was with the caliber of these people. Her response was, "Hilaire, this isn't Hollywood! These people are not the usual trip. They aren't sleeping around. They're in bed by 10 PM. No one is taking cocaine. These are beautiful people but this is not a typical Hollywood production!"

Kate always makes me feel a little naïve but I don't mind. She added, "It's hard to be beautiful in Hollywood. Damn hard. You have to be so strong!"

I had no idea how much planning and difficult hours go into a movie. They are very serious about their technique. It is more of a craft for these people than a job. Many of the cast and crew were working on the set before 5:30 AM. The light and sound crews were perfectionists. I took it all in.

I especially like C.B. "Duke" Cosgrove, the man in charge of Kate's trailer. Kept on location, it was a place for her to practice lines, reflect on characterization, to rest in or to stay away from photographers, autograph seekers, etc. Duke has been employed for years by ABC to take care of the stars. His favorites included Jackie Gleason, Danny Thomas, and Burt Reynolds.

One evening Duke and I were having dinner and the heel broke off my shoe. Kate and Jean LeClerc (who played Fr. Brute) had joined us. Kate turned to Duke, "Aren't you going to help Sister? Buy her a new pair of shoes, Duke!"

I interrupted, "Kate, I really don't need a new pair. I already have two others back in Lorain."

Kate looked surprised and laughed heartily as she admitted to having between 200 and 250 pair of shoes! "But Hilaire," she added, "I really have a thing about hats! I have between 60 and 75 of them!"

I thought about my two veils (one of which needs mending). It was all so funny. Kate and I, so different from each other, yet so much in tune.

The shooting one particular morning was very different for me. Rosalynn Carter's mother was on location with some of her very best friends. "Miss" Allie Smith is a small, frail, white-haired, delightful woman. [Little at the time did or could I suspect this would be the beginning of a twenty-year friendship with Miss Allie.]

Beverlee invited the foursome to dinner and a tour. The Georgians insisted we come to Plains, a short drive away. They showed us the sights of Plains, past security guards at the home of Jimmy and Rosalynn. Mrs. Smith impressed me as a dear, most lovely, sincere and gentle woman.

The entire week was a highlight but I remember with great fondness the day they filmed the death of Mrs. Seton. She doesn't actually die in the film but here is a scene where you know death is imminent. It was the last day of filming and everyone was quite drained, Kate especially. The cast and crew in general were eager to wrap it up.

Kate, as Mother Seton, lay in bed looking ghostly, pale and ravaged by a tubercular condition. Ken Chase did a marvelous job of making a vivacious 24-year old look like a dying 46-year old matron.

I was in the room across the hall. David Bernard, of the sound crew, gave me the earphones, which blocked out every sound except Kate's dying words. She was doing beautifully and I was deeply touched. Tears fell from my face into my lap.

Then in the middle of the scene Kate's stomach began to growl. The super sensitive microphone on her nightgown magnified the churning sounds into a gurgling roar.

Filming stopped. The director sent for a sandwich and a cup of coffee. Kate sat up in bed and downed half her meal in an attempt to stop the undesirable sound effects. By now my stomach had begun to do the same. It was past lunchtime and I hadn't bothered with breakfast. I knew a growling stomach was sufficient cause to have someone removed from the area. I didn't want to be asked to leave.

Then I spotted the half-finished sandwich and half cup of coffee. I asked Richard what would be done with it.

"We'll throw it away. Do you want it?"

I said, "Yes," and he told me to go right ahead and enjoy it. I did, over in a corner where the sound of my chewing would not be heard.

Fr. Joseph Dirvin, Miss Allie Smith (Rosalynn Carter's mom); Co-producers, Beverlee Dean and Jimmy Hawkins of "A Time for Miracles" and Sr. Mary Hilaire in front. Taken on location, February, 1980.

I felt much better. The director called for the other half of the sandwich. I overheard "Sister" being whispered several times and asked if I had done something wrong. They assured me it was all right, and there would be a lunch break for everyone. People were too eager, too tense, too hungry and too tired to finish everything just now. After the break the filming was completed.

Kate and I shared so much that week. I felt as if we had exchanged spiritual protoplasm, if there is such a thing. This was when I first spoke with Kate's mother on the phone. She asked me, "Sister, can you get my daughter into a convent?" Mrs. Mulgrew's humor was equal to Kate's. I thought fast. "I think that is something only God can arrange."

Kate is one of eight children in a very Irish and very Catholic family from Dubuque, Iowa. A month after filming she took her mother on a vacation to Italy. They are the best of friends.

So many people helped to make the film a masterpiece. I believe it can be a classic for years to come. Other stars include Lorne Green as Bishop John Carroll, Rosanno Brazzi as Philipo Filicchi, Leonard Mann as Antonio Filicchi, John Forsythe as Postulator of the Cause, Nan Mason as Sister Rose White, Milo O'Shea as Father O'Brien, Robin Clarke as William Seton Sr., Hoolian Burke as Sr. Maria Murphy, Jean Pierre Aumont as Fr. Dubois, Michael Higgins as Dr. Bayley, and Jean LeClerc as Father Brute.

People like Henry Denker, Michael O'Herlihy, Beverlee Dean, Jimmy Hawkins, Kate, Fred Karlin (music composer), Duke Cosgrove, Edie Panda, and countless others have created a film well worth our watching. It was a happy privilege to have been a small part of it.

The original title, "Mother Seton" was changed later to "A Time for Miracles." "A Time for Miracles" was certainly one for me.

CHAPTER TEN

Carl Hartman Jr.

After my ten day visit with the cast and crew of "A Time for Miracles," I returned to Lorain. I was thrilled that Sr. Rose Alice, my substitute for the week, was given $100.00 in payment for teaching my students. Sr. Rose Alice was pleased as well. In those days Sisters were rarely compensated for extra duty.

While teaching in Lorain I established a high school club and was particularly fond of Cindy Ernst and Carl Hartman, two of my leaders. They were a fun pair of kids. I also taught them religion class. I enjoyed teaching about the saints, and I remember Carl thinking it was pretty cool that anyone could be a saint; even he could. Cindy was one of my bus pilgrims to the Shrine of Mother Seton in Emmitsburg, and both of them developed a particular interest in and love for Mrs. Seton. She bought Carl a medal of Mother Seton at the shrine and he wore it everyday.

Shortly after my return from the Georgia trip Carl Jr. came to visit me. This high school senior wanted to know all about my filming adventures. He was the only one I recall who went out of his way to sit with me for several hours and ask about my visit to the Mother Seton movie. We sat together in one of the front convent parlors and talked up a storm. Carl wasn't a big conversationalist, so I found it interesting that he would do this.

Carl was an exceptional basketball player. His father, Carl Hartman Sr., was a coach at Lorain High School and to this day is greatly respected and admired in our Lorain community. Over the next few years Carl and Cindy continued to be the best of friends, and they included me.

In the spring of 1983 I was given an "obedience" to teach in Tampa, Florida. I was to leave in August so I decided to have a special mass in honor of Mother

Seton held in Columbia Station, about fifteen miles from home. Columbia Station had a church named in honor of St. Elizabeth Ann Seton.

I invited the pilgrims who had gone to Emmitsburg with me over the past five years and we planned a luncheon after the liturgy. About 200 pilgrims attended, and we all seemed to enjoy the event. A friend of mine at the time, Anita Clark, wanted to visit Emmitsburg with me, and I wanted to return to Emmitsburg once more before my assignment to Florida. I felt the far greater distance from the shrine would mean less opportunity to visit.

It was decided that Anita and I would drive, on August 10th just after the Mother Seton mass in Columbia Station, to Emmitsburg. Cindy was at the mass but Carl wasn't. By now he and Cindy had decided to separate and get to know other people, making new friends. Carl was attending college at Baldwin Wallace and playing basketball for them. When I look back, I'm pretty sure they were each other's first true love. I know Cindy found the breakup difficult but they both parted as friends.

As Anita and I drove to Emmitsburg after the mass we were feeling excited about the trip ahead of us. We had arranged to get Sr. Frances Anne Odum and several other Daughters of Charity who lived with her at the Provincial House then drive them to their convent in Martinsburg, West Virginia. They were on retreat in Emmitsburg and Anita and I had offered to be their "taxi" back to their convent.

When we arrived in E-burg it was getting dark. I asked Anita if she would be willing to go up to Mount St. Mary's Grotto before we checked in the motel. I told her I had been on the mountain every time of day but never at night. She was fine with the idea and so we approached the mountain road. There was a gate down preventing us from driving further up the road. We parked the car and walked in the twilight.

We walked past the cemetery to our left and then past the Pangborn Memorial. Now we had another problem. The gate to the Grotto was locked. We looked for a path around the gate and nearly stepped off a cliff in the darkness. We decided to take the direct approach and scale the fifteen-foot iron gate. I had never known Anita to wear a dress and it was ironic and amusing that she did that day.

Next we walked up the asphalt path to the grotto. There was sufficient light for us to see. When we got to the grotto, we separated. She prayed in the mountain bleachers, and I sat on the stone railing near the statue of Our Lady. We both had lots of praying to do. My mind was filled with people and intentions.

After fifteen or twenty minutes we retraced our path, climbing back over the gate, walking past Pangborn Memorial and the cemetery, now to our right. We could see the streetlight below and our parked car. The light from the sky gave just enough light that we could stay on the road.

Then suddenly, from the right, a speck of light down the road a ways, leapt into the center of the street and proceeded to approach us. As it came closer it got larger until it spontaneously diffused into multiple rays, all shining in many directions. It was as if we were at some great intersection of cars with laser-like headlights, beaming in every direction. It approached us quickly, and then almost as quickly contracted into a speck of light once more, and leapt to the left side of the road in front of us.

I was the first to speak. "Anita! Did you see that?"

"Yeah," she answered.

"What was it?" I asked.

"I think it was a deer," she replied.

"A deer?" I could not believe what she said. But just then there was a rustling of sound to the left of me. I thought perhaps something was about to leap from the left side of the road, and I made the sign of the cross. I thought I might be consumed or attacked by the bizarre, intense white light.

Instead I glanced to see that Anita, who was walking to the right of me, stepped behind me and now approached from my left. She said, "It's on this side of the road; it will get me first."

Yes, that blew my mind. The two of us picked up our pace and were relieved to safely reach the car and drive off the mountain.

We didn't talk about it that night before going to bed. I'm not sure why, but I don't recall that we did. I do remember the conversation we had the next morning.

"Anita, what did you see on the mountain last night?"

"Hilaire, it was some kind of strange light. It was coming at us and burst into a whole lot of lights. I thought it was going to get us."

"Then why did you say you thought it was a deer?"

"I have no idea. It was the dumbest thing I ever said. I have no idea why I said that."

Well, that was a relief. At least I had not been the only one to see the strange light on Mt. St. Mary's. After breakfast we went to the shrine for a visit, then to the Provincial House to get the three nuns we were taking to Martinsburg, West Virginia. I was looking forward to seeing Sr. Frances Anne. Anita, Sr. Frances and I were planning a day trip to Harper's Ferry the next day.

Upon greeting the nuns, two of whom were maybe 20 or 30 years older, I asked them if they had ever heard of strange lights on Mount St. Mary's. They said that they hadn't. I was still so bothered by what Anita and I had seen that I continued to talk about it on the way to their convent. I could not understand why we would experience something so extraordinary. I have generally espoused the belief that there is a reason for everything, so why did we see what we saw? It bothered me.

The next day we spent touring Harper's Ferry as planned, but after returning to the convent Anita and I were rather tired, and the nuns encouraged us to stay one more night with them. I called my mother to tell her our plans had changed and we would not be returning to Lorain until the next day.

"I was hoping you'd come back tonight," Mom said. That surprised me because Mother seldom suggested I change my plans. I knew there was a reason.

"Why, Mom?"

"Carl Hartman committed suicide."

I was shocked beyond words. "Senior or Junior?" I asked.

"The young man, Carl."

She knew little more than that, and the wake was to be the next morning.

"Mom, Anita and I are putting our things in the car. We're coming home tonight. I need to call Cindy and see how she is. I'll call you when I get to Lorain."

All of the Sisters understood the situation. It was about a six-hour drive and we would get to Lorain after midnight, but Anita and I both knew it was important to get back. I called Cindy and she asked if I would stay with her that night. I told her I would.

As Anita and I drove across the PA turnpike I had an insight. The light on the mountain had bothered me ever since it happened. I thought out loud, "Anita, I wonder if that light we saw on the mountain had something to do with Carl Hartman's death."

All of a sudden in the dark sky before us there appeared a bird shape made of that same brilliant white light Anita and I had seen on the mountain in Emmitsburg. It was about to fly into our windshield, but when there should have been contact there was nothing.

"Anita. Did you see that?"

She laughed. "Hilaire, I'm never coming to Emmitsburg with you again! What was it, a bird made of light? You were going to hit it and the thing just disappeared."

That dove-like figure was my confirmation. "Anita. I get it. If that light on the mountain has anything to do with Carl Hartman's death, it will all make sense."

It wasn't until I was with Cindy that I learned Carl had died the same day at approximately the same time we saw the light on the mountain. Carl had taken his life at James Day Park with his grandfather's rifle.

The following morning Cindy and I attended the funeral. Carl and Nancy Hartman were glad to see me, and Carl Sr. took my hand. He placed me next to him and would not let go. They were so obviously shattered.

Carl Hartman, Jr.
March 20, 1962-August 10, 1983

At the end of that mournful service, the coffin needed to be closed. People from the back of the room began the process of final farewells, filing past Carl's mortal remains. Mr. and Mrs. Hartman and Carl's family approached last. Nancy and I literally had to help hold Mr. Hartman up. He sobbed with intense grief. We guided him into an adjacent room while the coffin was being closed. I had no idea if it was the right time to say something. I was torn. Still, I decided to tell Carl what I had seen in Emmitsburg while his son was dying.

Carl listened attentively and became composed. Then he asked if I would join him and Nancy in their car for the ride to the funeral mass at St. Anthony's. I was comforted to be with them. Carl continued to hold my hand. I prayed desperately for their consolation.

After mass there was a meal at the social hall. I explained to Carl's mom and dad that I was leaving for Florida the next day and I probably would not be able to see them again until Christmas. They were deeply grateful for my support. In all of that what truly amazed me was the way Carl had managed to go from obviously tormented to amazing composure.

I wouldn't understand why until Carl sent me a letter in Florida.

I will paraphrase his letter. Carl wrote, "Hilaire, when the police officer came to my home to tell me what had happened, the first thought I had was, 'God, if you will only give me a sign that my son is with you, that he is all right, I will find a way to cope.'"

"Sister, I don't know why you were given the sign I asked for but when you told me what you had seen in Emmitsburg I just knew God had sent you the sign I prayed for; he gave it to you. I don't know how Nancy and I will cope but I believe we will find the grace to accept what we must."

The following year Carl, Nancy, and their youngest son Mike went to Emmitsburg with Anita and me. We explained all of the events of that evening and when the Hartmans returned to Lorain, Nancy told me that they were all greatly helped by their pilgrimage.

It was during that visit I made with the Hartmans that I realized the grotto needed a wheelchair. Many pilgrims came with their own but there were others who wanted to go up the path to the grotto but could not negotiate the incline. That's when I got the idea to purchase a wheelchair in memory of Carl. During 1984-85, about 300 people donated $1.00 each to get the chair. Monsignor Hugh J. Phillips was very grateful and made all the arrangements.

So is this all just coincidental? I don't think so. I don't think Cindy giving Carl a medal of Mother Seton, Carl having a devotion to Mother Seton, the light on the mountain, or the wheelchair was anything but life unfolding. Over the years in my own heart of hearts, Carl Hartman Jr. has been my personal patron saint of suicide. Carl had confided that he liked the idea of becoming a saint.

When it comes to suicide, I don't believe any of us can judge. There is still much science to be done. It is a chemical imbalance. These people are in a torment so great that only death appears the best resolve. Suicide is a permanent solution to a temporary problem.

I'm almost sixty now and I have lived to witness an epidemic of young people taking their own lives before they had a chance to live. Is some of this induced by drug use? Yes. Are thoughts of suicide brought on by despair, emotional, or physical pain? Yes. Does this happen in healthy families to people who have everything to life for? Yes. It's easy to speculate underlying causes but impossible to know with absolute certainty exactly why it happens.

I often pray to Carl for young people. He knew that torment. He kept it inside yet acted upon the pain. Cindy told me Carl had spoken of suicide but she never for a moment thought he could ever really consider it.

Like Mr. and Mrs. Hartman, Mother Seton knew the sorrow of burying a child. In fact two of her daughters preceded her in death. The life of St. Elizabeth Ann Seton is a wonderful source of comfort for parents who have experienced this immeasurable sorrow. The saints are our friends as much if not more than those who love us in this world. The difference is, saints who have gone before us have a different perspective in heaven. They understand that our suffering here will melt into everlasting joy once we return to God.

I wanted to tell you about Carl Hartman Jr. because I believe he is one of Mother Seton's friends. I'm grateful he was one of mine.

Postscript: I really had no idea when Carl's birthday was when I wrote this chapter, but "coincidentally", I delivered this story to the Hartman family home on March 20th, 2008, Carl Jr.'s birthday. He died 25 years ago in 1983.

CHAPTER ELEVEN

After the Movie

After I worked on "A Time for Miracles" and did all I could to help promote the film, I was sent from my home parish in Lorain to Incarnation Convent in Tampa, Florida. I had a very difficult year living in that convent. And for some reason I didn't promote Mother Seton there. I think I felt, "She's been canonized; there are lots of books about her; they've even made a movie about her life." I thought my work was done.

After one year in Tampa I was sent to teach English in Puerto Rico. I didn't want to go to Puerto Rico and told Sr. Aileen that I had failed my second year of Spanish in high school. That didn't seem to matter, and so I went as ordered and lasted three months. I was isolated and felt wronged, angry, and depressed. I left the convent on October 28, 1984, the Feast of St. Jude. I guess I was one of those impossible cases.

After that I decided to live in Tampa. I taught there and earned a doctorate from the University of South Florida. I stayed for ten years but never gave a talk on Mrs. Seton and may have visited the shrine once or twice while spending time with Mom in Ohio. My contact with Ann O'Neill lessened as she was going through painful marital problems, and it was difficult for me to share in her struggle.

My bond with Rosalynn Carter's mother, Miss Allie, became stronger and we increasingly stayed in touch. I think there were a few years when I called her every Sunday. Kate Mulgrew and I had no contact after I left the convent except for one letter she sent with photographs of her two sons.

My relationships with Sr. Mary Ruth Morrill, Sr. Sylvia Borden and Sr. Frances Anne Odum all continued, in spite of the fact all three Daughters of Charity had left Mother Seton's community.

One summer, driving to Lorain from Tampa, I contacted Mary Ruth Morrill Smith, now married with two children, and told her I would love to stop and see her in Hendersonville, North Carolina while en route to Ohio. She and her husband offered a weekend of hospitality. It was an amazing reunion. Mary Ruth had distanced our relationship for years and now I was invited to their home.

I remember arriving while Mary Ruth and the children were at mass. Her husband Edward was waiting at their summer lake home to take me to the little mountain Catholic church where they worshipped. The children were keyed in to go with Daddy when I arrived so that Mary Ruth and I could have some alone time.

I felt very emotional and recall that during mass I actually had tears. Mary Ruth reached out and touched me, assuring me everything would be fine. After mass I met their priest and we walked to my car. I wanted to know immediately why she felt it necessary to not be in my life all those years. She told me I would have to wait just a little while longer to know.

That evening while Mary Ruth read to the children and put them to bed, Edward and I sat on the screen porch visiting. When Mary Ruth came in he excused himself with, "Well, I know you gals have some things to talk about."

I don't need to go into details, but simply, Mary Ruth told me that at that time in her life she was not comfortable with anyone trying to love her. She told me, "Hilaire, when you love someone, they know it. You were like a freight train, a Mack truck, when you came into my life! I really did not know how to accept your love."

"But you had no problem accepting Edward's."

"Edward slowly, almost imperceptibly, came into my heart. It was very different. But I'm not the same person I was years ago and I really want to have you in my life with my husband and children."

I was so grateful. Over the years since then Mary Ruth and I have visited together in Florida, in Lorain, in Dayton at her sister's home, and other places as well. We have had many long, meaningful conversations. I am so grateful that the individual who led me to my friendship with Mrs. Seton is so comfortable and direct with me now. We are only a phone call away from each other. Over the years I have been aware from a distance that her children have grown into wonderful adults. Mary Ruth is one of the chapters in my life that greatly improved.

In 1993, I finished my doctorate and moved back to Lorain to be with my mother. I gave one talk on Mother Seton, but there just wasn't the same kind of interest within me to promote and teach her life. Mother Seton became a quiet friend. She was still in my life but there was no longer this compelling need to promote her. I continued to believe she loved me.

In December of 1994 I found myself fighting with the school superintendent and other Lorainites to save our local high school. Lorain High School was my alma mater. It had more than 130 years of illustrious tradition, and our superintendent wanted to close the happiest, most productive, oldest, (and to my prejudicial thinking), best high school in Lorain. There were two other high schools, but student enrollment was dropping, and the board of education was planning to keep the 30 and 40 year-old schools open and close Lorain High.

It was a very stressful time for me. I was home writing books and helping Mom in any way I could. She had acute emphysema and was homebound by now. I attended the public forums to fight the decision to close our high school, and one evening I was in the kitchen and walked through the dining into the living room. It was the strangest thing ever.

Mother was sitting on the couch and in the middle of the room, I sensed that Mother Seton was there with the Blessed Mother. I know that is impossible to explain and I really can't explain it. It was as if I could see them, but I couldn't. I just **knew** they were there. And even more strangely I knew that Mrs. Seton had brought or invited the Mother of Jesus. It wasn't the other way around. The good news is I don't have to prove anything. It just happened that way. I'm at a loss to describe the experience.

Immediately I sensed that I needed to go to Emmitsburg. I said to my mother, "Mom, I need to drive over to Emmitsburg for a weekend. Is that okay with you?" She was fine with it. Mother was the least interfering person I ever knew. She was the epitome of live and let live. So by the following weekend I was on my way to the shrine.

I remember that when I got there, I checked into my room at the Provincial House and then went directly to the altar where her relic remains are kept. I found myself in a torrent of tears, sharing every concern within my soul with Elizabeth. This went on for quite a while and I explained to my dear friend the battle to save Lorain High School. I had become so very invested in that cause.

Eventually the torment subsided and a peace came over me. It was amazing. The rest of my stay was pleasant and uneventful, but I do know that when I returned to Lorain I had a new resolve. I had acceptance of what I could not change. It was inevitable and it did happen. 1995 was the last graduation class for Lorain High. My nephew Jeremy would have to spend his senior year at Admiral King High School. He would have been the fourth generation in our family to graduate from Lorain High, but it didn't happen.

However, that experience did assure me all the more that my friendship with Mrs. Seton was still very viable. In 1995 I wrote a story for the Syracuse, *Catholic Sun* as I realized there were millions of people who had forgotten about St. Elizabeth Ann Seton, and millions more who have never heard of her. 1995 marked twenty years since her canonization and the following chapter is the story I published back then.

One of many pilgrimage groups that Sr. Mary Hilaire led to the Shrine of Mother Seton in Emmitsburg. Her mother is on the far left, front row.

CHAPTER TWELVE

The Only American-born Saint

REFLECTING ON ST. ELIZABETH ANN SETON, WHO WAS CANONIZED 20 YEARS AGO THIS WEEK.

Why is it that Americans will do almost anything to obtain earthly treasures, when logistically, earthly riches cannot be taken with us from this world? What we do take is the legacy of our choices, how we have chosen to live. Interestingly it is also what we leave behind.

We all need good examples, role models, inspiring people in our lives to challenge our complacency and mediocrity. Perhaps if we look to our parents, grandparents, teachers, neighbors or friends, we may be fortunate enough to discover that which truly enriches. Without question heroic qualities are always present in the lives of our saints, canonized and uncanonized.

St. Elizabeth Ann Seton, America's only native-born saint, was a faithful wife, a devoted mother, an attentive daughter, a loyal friend, a compassionate socialite, a fervent Episcopalian, a confirmed Roman Catholic, an extraordinary teacher, a pioneering foundress, a brave and faith-centered woman. She desired to be a channel of grace and love for all who entered her life. Imagine a world where we all shared such ambition!

Has her canonization affected anyone? Has the proclamation by Pope Paul VI on September 14, 1975 changed anything? I think so. Perhaps it has encouraged some of us to become saints; perhaps it has given our nation, our world, a much-needed dose of hope and edification. There are many of us who require the example of leadership to become leaders.

By 1978, three years after Mother Seton's canonization, there were 88 religious institutions (churches, schools, hospitals, etc.) in American bearing Mother Seton's name. Today that number has greatly increased. Dozens of books are being written about her and hundreds of thousands of pilgrims (including former President Carter and Mother Teresa of Calcutta) have visited the Shrine of St. Elizabeth Ann Seton in Emmitsburg, MD. Everyone who comes to know her life and example cannot be unaffected.

As a young woman, Elizabeth Ann Bayley, born an Episcopalian in 1774, was active in the Society for Destitute Women. She married William Magee Seton in 1794 and together they had five children.

After her husband died in 1803 in Italy, she returned to the United States where she converted and entered the Catholic faith. In 1808 she moved her family to Baltimore, opened a school for girls, and soon took religious vows.

She began forming aspirants for the sisterhood and established a convent and school in Emmitsburg, MD, from which grew the present Daughters of Charity Province. From her foundation grew seven separate religious congregations. Her labors began the American parochial school system. She died in 1821.

The process of canonization for Mother Seton spanned 72 years. It formally began in 1882 and finished in 1975. The process required that three authenticated, documented, scientifically-investigated miracles be attributed to her intercession and celestial status.

Mother Seton is credited with the cure of Sister Gertrude Korzendorfer's cancerous pancreas in 1935. Sister Korzendorfer was a Daughter of Charity who served as administrator and superior of a 250 bed hospital for the insane in New Orleans. Eight years after her cure she died of a heart attack. The autopsy revealed no cancer.

Ann Teresa O'Neill was cured of lymphatic leukemia in 1952 when she was 4 ½ years old. It was 12 years before Rome declared the cure miraculous. O'Neill attended the beatification ceremony of Mother Seton in Rome, when she was 15, on St. Patrick's Day, March 17, 1963. She and her mother returned to Rome for Mother Seton's canonization along with the third miracle cure, Carl Eric Kalin.

Kalin suffered from rubeola and fulminating meningeo encephalitis, red measles and inflammation of the brain. Kalin was a Lutheran but his wife, a Catholic, placed a relic of Mother Seton on his comatose body. That afternoon in 1963, he came out of the coma and was dismissed from the hospital. (A year after the canonization he died from prostate cancer.)

The Vatican generally requires four miracles for sainthood but Pope Paul VI waived the fourth so that Mother Seton could be canonized during the Holy Year and the International Year of the Woman.

To me it seems the ultimate accomplishment, to be a saint, to seek to become the instrument of God's mercy and justice while growing older, preparing for the next experience of life. Today too many of us live with earthly goals. We neglect to live for heaven. Scripture reminds us, "Wherever your treasure lies, there your heart will be." (Luke, 12:34)

At the age of 26 I represented the Sisters of St. Francis of Syracuse at the canonization of Mother Seton. At that time, I was a member of their community. I have since spent many years researching, writing and teaching the life and example of Mother Seton.

I was a student at Catholic University in Washington, D.C., during the summer of 1971 when I first learned of Mother Seton. At the age of 21 I met Sr. Mary Ruth Morrill, a Daughter of Charity, who aroused my curiosity about this married mother of five, community foundress. Sister Morrill provided me with Fr. Dirvin's book, *Mrs. Seton*. I read it in two days, both laughing and crying aloud. I would never be the same.

I think the life and example of St. Elizabeth Ann Bayley Seton just seems to affect people that way. When we personally know Christ and those who imitate His way, we have to be changed. Love imposes an improvement upon every human condition.

CHAPTER THIRTEEN

What Next?

Who of any of us can possibly know what is next? I imagine I will live another score or so of years, and will Mother Seton continue to inspire and operate within my life? I hope so. I look back over the past 40 years and admit that most of my highlights were related to a person I never actually met. I think that unusual. I can't explain or understand it, but I am grateful.

I have been to many of the places Mother Seton walked, lived, worked or places strongly related to her life. I've been to New York City, Baltimore, Emmitsburg, Livorno, Italy. I've been to her motherhouses in Cincinnati, OH, Greensburg, PA, Riverdale, New York, but have not as yet been to Convent Station or Halifax. I've researched in Philadelphia and rediscovered the grave of her dearest friend, Juliana Sitgreaves Scott.

I've given hundreds of talks on Mother Seton's life, published stories about her life, led hundreds of pilgrims to Emmitsburg, and been there myself at least 40 times. I've attended her canonization, worked as a script consultant and advisor for the ABC-TV docudrama "A Time for Miracles" and befriended people like Annabelle Melville, Fr. Dirvin, Ann O'Neill and her family, Fr. Sylvester A. Taggart, Msgn. Phillips, Fr. Jack Lombardi, Sr. Isabel Tooey, Sr. Theresa Kane, RSM, Don Gino Franchi, and direct descendents of the Filicchi family, particularly Francesca Quaratesi, great-great-granddaughter of Antonio and Amabilia Filicchi. I've known and loved several of Mother Seton's spiritual daughters, Mary Ruth Morrill Smith, Sylvia Borden Mace, Frances Anne Odum, Sr. Mary Ellen Sheldon, Sr. Eleanor McNabb, and others. I've met movie stars, bishops and cardinals, and people like the Jimmy Carter family. What an amazing privilege it has all been.

Mother Seton's House, 600 N. Paca Street, Baltimore, MD. Mother Seton lived here from 1808-1809.

Around five years ago when Sylvia Borden Mace was visiting my home with her husband Richard, she told me she had seen Mother Seton in my bedroom mirror when she awoke one morning. Anything is possible. The only vision I've had of Mother Seton was one where I could not actually see her, only a knowing that she was there, standing in our Alexander Avenue living room.

I have no idea if you will find my stories helpful or inspiring. I know the story of Mrs. Seton's life has been a wonderful, profound influence in my life. But I also hope that her canonization will not distance Mrs. Seton from your coming to know her personally. She had real-world problems, losing her mom at such an early age, a baby sister dying, and a distant father. Her life with her stepmother was anything but ideal, and endless struggles with her husband's health, conversion, raising her children, etc. When her sons did write her from a distance, it was often to ask for money. Mother Seton is someone with whom we can all find something in common. As for anything I ever may have done to help others come to know her it seems as if I have only received, because the joy of sharing her was so meaningful.

In November of 2007 I drove to Baltimore, MD to visit Ann O'Neill's mother and her sister Jeanne. I went there to interview Mrs. O'Neill, now 85 years old. I wanted to record her personal memories of Ann's miraculous cure, and she was gracious as ever to share them.

I have decided to close this book with the story Mrs. O'Neill has given us. It comes from one of the greatest believers I've ever known. Writing this book has been my attempt to tie together many loose ends. I cannot guarantee my work is error-free as I have never known me to do anything perfectly. I have done my best and I hope you will benefit from my efforts.

My goal is to have the book finished before June 15th of 2008 as that is the date they are planning to celebrate the 200th anniversary of Mrs. Seton arriving in Baltimore. (Actually this is the date I finished my completed manuscript.) Many will also be celebrating the bicentennial anniversary of the dedication of the Old Sulpician Seminary Chapel on Paca Street as Mrs. Seton arrived during the dedication mass of that church. Elizabeth came to Baltimore as Mrs. Seton and left for Emmitsburg a year later as Mother Seton. She took her religious vows in the lower chapel of the Old Sulpician St. Mary's Seminary Chapel.

May Saint Elizabeth Ann Bayley Seton bless you and yours; may she watch over our nation and our world with the same love and fervor she had for her family, her children, her students, her spiritual daughters, her friends and her God. May she and all the saints one day welcome each of us home once more into her dearest "Eternity".

CHAPTER FOURTEEN

"Get to the Saints, Mother!
Get to the Saints!"

I have come to believe that the essence of living has everything to do with relationship. The substance of relationship is reciprocation, giving and receiving, modes of both expression and reception. Say it any way you may like but it is the glue of our connectedness that keeps us viable.

Just as the relationship I had with my parents connected me all the more to my grandparents, the relationship I have with my siblings connects me all the more to their children. I feel the same is true of our friends. If you are a friend to my friend I have a connection with you. I think this is true of the saints as well. They all know each other and celebrate the love they have for each other while enjoying the bliss of God's loving presence in heaven. I think someone might have put it this way: "Any friend of God is a friend of mine."

When I began this book about my friendship with Mother Seton I realized that even though I have my own personal bond with Mrs. Seton, I am connected with her through numerous other relationships as well, particularly through Ann Teresa O'Neill.

Ann O'Neill was the recipient of a miracle. At the age of four and a half she received a documented leukemia cure that is worthy of a book itself. When I think of Ann I think of Mother Seton, and when I think of Mother Seton I think of Ann. They are profoundly connected in relationship. I'm quite sure Mrs. Seton knew whom she would be helping when the miracle transpired and I believe Ann was chosen for this purpose.

I first met Ann in Rome at the Hotel Leonardo DiVinci while attending the canonization of St. Elizabeth Ann Seton in September of 1975. I had known a good deal about her and the miracle she received before our meeting, but as Ann will tell you this was a unique and memorable encounter for us both when we met. It was through Ann that I came to know her mother, Mrs. Felixena Phelps O'Neill, and her four sisters, Jeanne, Mary Margaret, Celine and Theresa.

In November of 2007 I went to Baltimore and stayed with Mrs. O'Neill, her daughter Jeanie, son-in-law Steve, and granddaughter Natalie so that I might interview Mrs. O'Neill about that time in 1952 when the saints came to her assistance. I knew that I wanted Mrs. O'Neill's remembrances of that time to be a chapter in this book. After countless tellings, Mrs. O'Neill was patient and kind enough to retell the story of Ann's miraculous cure again:

"It was late one February evening in 1952 and my husband and I were expecting our third child at nearly any time. We were living in a little stone Cape Cod house that William had built for us and we had two little girls. Ann Teresa was nearly four and a half and her little sister, Jeanne Marie, was two and a half. We were living on Rockridge Road in Pikesville and I felt content with our home and our family life.

"That very evening I noticed that while Ann and Jeanne were playing, Ann was not herself. She was acting irritable. Then I noticed the blood blotches on her skin and I felt immediate concern. As soon as possible we took Ann to the family doctor and he had her blood count taken. I recall them reporting a low number of 43. Now I was even more concerned.

"That night I began a novena to the Infant Jesus. I had a statue of the Infant of Prague and every hour, all night long for nine hours, I would awake and say the prayer. I woke every hour in time for the novena and then returned to sleep."

"We needed to put Ann in St. Agnes Hospital as they had to give her blood transfusions, but her blood vessels would not hold the fresh blood. I was expecting my third daughter and the doctors did not want to tell me that Ann had leukemia. My husband explained that Ann needed to be transferred to University Hospital. At the time I did not realize this was a research hospital and that children there were used to help find a cause and cure of this awful disease.

"When I went to see Ann, it was so pitiful a sight. She had bruises all over her. 'Look what they are doing to me, Mother. Take me home!' she pleaded. They were sponging her, trying to break the fever. It would break any mother's heart.

"I had to leave Ann at University Hospital and return to St. Agnes to give birth to my baby. I asked the Blessed Mother for help and in gratitude, I changed the name we had planned for her from Margaret Mary to Mary Margaret. I put Our Lady's name first, before the name of Margaret, because Our Blessed Mother helped me through this very difficult experience.

"I was permitted to recover from giving birth at St. Agnes at the University Hospital so that I could be near Ann. Mary Margaret came home with me for only a few days so that I could prepare her to stay with my aunt. Mary Margaret was baptized at All Saints Church in Liberty Heights within a week or two of her birth and my Aunt Rita and Uncle Mac took care of her for us. My second daughter Jeanne was staying with my father and my Aunt Agnes, even though my sister-in-law wanted to take care of her.

"It was after the birth of Mary Margaret that the doctor told me Ann had leukemia. He also said that it has never been known in medical history that anyone had ever survived leukemia. He told me there was no hope in the world for Ann to live through this.

"More than once I would turn to my own dearly departed Mother in heaven and beg for her help. 'Get to the saints, Mother! Get to the saints!' I implored. I knew they were all together, and that Mother must certainly know someone there who could help us."

As I listened to Mrs. O'Neill speak passionately of these impressions, memories, and details of fifty-six years ago, she still related her experiences with much of the feeling she possessed even then. It made me think of my own dear mother and the countless times since her death in February of 1999 that I have turned to her for help and intercession. When in crisis I think it the most natural thing in the world to ask someone with whom we share a sacred, loving relationship to come to our aid.

"It was so difficult that my newborn needed to live at a distance. I was so torn, not being able to see her. It made me reflect upon the life of the mother of St. Therese of Lisieux, who had to give up her child for a while as she needed to recover her health and how it must have broken her heart to be separated. I found myself praying all of the time.

"I especially prayed to the Infant Jesus of Prague for guidance. I looked at others reading a daily newspaper and could not understand how they would spend their time reading the news when they could use this time to read and pray.

"When I returned to University Hospital after Mary Margaret was born, I was shocked to see how awful Ann looked. She had a big, white, swollen face, and her head was shaking constantly. This was so disturbing. My sister Ann Rita (whom we called Nancy) told me, 'But Sis, you didn't see her before! She is so much better now.'

"The doctors were very direct with me now. Dr. Milton Sacks, her Jewish leukemia specialist, was wonderful. He had a marvelous reputation, but he too did not want me to think Ann would survive. By now all believed that Ann would die, as back then, all children died of leukemia. But I could not and would not stop believing Ann would live.

"It took me a while to understand what a research hospital was like. Our family doctor confessed that if he knew what Ann would have to go through he would not have recommended she be put in the research center of University Hospital. They continuously used experimental drugs on the children, and they were hardened to it. They only cared about the research. There was this child with a big bandage on her head and I asked her mother what was wrong. The mother told me her daughter had leukemia. If the leukemia didn't kill the children the drugs would.

"Ann wasn't eating but one day she seemed a little improved. I thought she was going to eat for me, and a nurse came to snatch her up and take her down the hall. I said, 'Let her eat,' but my words fell upon deaf ears. Then I heard screams and I followed the voice. It sounded like Ann. They were giving her another transfusion and my baby was screaming because of the needles.

"My husband and I were beside ourselves with worry. Our hearts were in constant grief, as you can only imagine. We couldn't endure much more and we asked the doctor if we could just take Ann home with us. He agreed that there was really nothing more they could do for Ann but ordered one last eight-hour transfusion. Then we could take her home.

"They medicated her so she could rest and we stayed with her during the transfusion. The doctor told me to watch the blood drop and I literally could not take my eyes from it. I was very obedient. During this time, I wasn't very strong myself but I watched that transfusion take place until Ann became hysterical. That was it. My husband could not endure any more either. He told the intern, 'Just stop it!' and he did.

"We found sheets in a closet and carried our daughter home to die.

Mrs. O'Neill interrupted her story to tell me, "You know, Hilaire, there was a time when I could not talk about this. I would tremble." I was so grateful that she could find the resources to return to that most terrible time in her life. I knew that in sharing her story she would be helping others to deal with their own.

"Fr. Linus Robinson, the priest who helped us to bury my mother, came over to bless Ann. I knew him from St. Paul's Church in Ellicot City. That was where I first met him. He had driven from western Maryland to bless my daughter. There was another priest from St. Charles's who came to visit, from near Pikesville, maybe.

"Ann was gasping and my husband thought it might be a cold she may have gotten but the priest said, 'No, it's congestion.' Things were so critical now and it was getting impossible to give her any relief. The struggle was just too difficult to watch, so we took her back to St. Agnes Hospital. This just happened to be Holy Week.

"I recall on Holy Thursday how I asked God that my little girl would get well and walk one day in the Holy Eucharistic procession. I remembered how terrified the Blessed Mother must have felt when Jesus was lost in the Jewish Temple. I appealed to her as one mother to another and the anxiety she must have had . . . surely she understood my suffering as I tried to reflect upon hers.

"I just kept praying. It kept me calm. Everyone I knew felt I was misguided to believe God would heal Ann. I tried to tell my husband that Ann would get well but he could not believe it either. It was heartbreaking for both of us to see open sores all over Anne's head and body. She had chicken pox and leukemia.

"Ann was so bad on Good Friday. Now I found myself adding a new prayer. I told God that 'If you are not going to end the suffering of Ann and me, and if you are not going to heal her, and if saving her life would not save her soul, then may your holy will be accomplished. I will give her up with all the love in my heart but you are so powerful I know you can heal her and I cannot stop pleading that you will!'" If a miracle was not in God's plan, then Mrs. O'Neill pleaded that God please end Ann's suffering and take her to heaven.

"On Easter Sunday my father came to see us in the hospital and he told me, 'Nothing looks like anything is going to save her now.' My father left the hospital very unhappy. Not just because of his granddaughter's condition but probably just as sad that I could not give up my hope and my belief that Ann would survive this. Then my brother came 'Come on now, Sis,' he told me, trying to get me to be realistic.

"That evening Sr. Mary Alice Fowler stopped in to talk with me. Sister was a Daughter of Charity who was in charge of the children's ward. I had spoken with her before but on this evening she came to explain to me that her mother foundress, Elizabeth Ann Seton, was being considered for beatification.

"I had never heard of Mother Seton before, but I listened carefully as Sister explained that there had been a miracle in 1939; a nun had been cured of pancreatic cancer through the intercession of Mother Seton. Sister also explained that if there were a second miracle Rome would honor their mother foundress by proclaiming her Blessed Elizabeth Ann Seton. However, a miracle was required, a miracle such as the cure of little Ann Teresa. The situation, to be considered a miracle, had to be as hopeless and impossible as this. Sr. Mary Alice told me, 'This will take great faith,' and I replied, 'Sister, I have the faith.'"

"Sister gave me prayer cards and I began to pass them out. I wanted to entrust Ann to the intercession of Mother Seton. I called Fr. Robinson and asked him to join in my prayers to Mrs. Seton. I told him what had happened and I remember saying to him, 'But Father, I know she's going to get well!' He replied, 'Oh, God bless you! You make me feel so little.' I said, 'Oh, Father!' because in my eyes, he was such a great and holy soul.

"I called my Aunt Agnes to tell her and she was furious with me. That I had this hope! I told her, 'It's love Aunt Ag. The love of Jesus and his mother.' In that moment I felt that love, and I would not let anything disturb me. Aunt Agnes felt I should be told of my delusions.

"When I called Aunt Rita she became upset with her sister, Aunt Agnes, for speaking so harshly with me. For a while they weren't even talking with each other. There was so much tension in the family at that time.

"After Easter, Ann seemed to get a little stronger. She could even stand. I asked one of her doctors at St. Agnes if we could possibly take Ann to Emmitburg, Maryland, to the burial place of Mother Seton. Sister Mary Alice was excited about the prospect but my own sister Ann Rita ("Nancy") was deeply disturbed with the idea. 'You're not taking that child up there in that condition.' I told my sister, 'Nancy, there is nothing that can hurt her now, given the circumstances. With what she has, what can hurt her now?'

"We took her up on a crib mattress. I even stopped to get an umbrella as it was raining." Mrs. O'Neill laughed at the absurdity of being worried about a little water when her daughter had acute lymphatic leukemia. "We took her to the Mortuary Chapel. We prayed and asked once more for a miracle.

"After the visit to the tomb of Mother Seton, we returned to Baltimore and for another blood test."

Sr. Mary Alice was the one to call Mrs. O'Neill. "Ann's blood has built up! It's normal! It's better than mine is," she had exclaimed! The miracle was said to be instantaneous. Mrs. O'Neill had received her miracle.

"When Ann was 12, the Roman Curia first requested that she have a bone marrow test to prove there were no hiding leukocytes in her body. Fr. Burgio accompanied us. [At that time, the Vice Postulator for the Cause was Rev. Salvator Burgio, C.M.] I didn't think the test was necessary, but they insisted, and it was very painful. There were several bone marrow tests, both in Baltimore and in Boston. It was difficult trying to assure the church hierarchy that a miracle had transpired.

"I had to appear before a tribunal. There were lots of priests all around me, sitting in two tiers as I sat at a table in the midst of them. I had to kneel and take an oath to tell the truth. Dr. Sacks had to testify that something like this has never ever happened before. He wouldn't say that it was a miracle. He said that you could call it whatever you like, but it has never happened before.

"No doctor would ever say that Ann was cured. Even though no one could explain what happened, I knew it was a miracle. There was a lot of tension in that room too, and I especially realized when I told them, 'Not everyone believes in miracles.' When I told them that, I heard this collective sigh of relief coming from these men.

"My husband and Sr. Mary Alice also had to testify for the tribunal, and we were forbidden to discuss our remarks with each other. We were told to keep all of this in confidence."

Ann turned 60 years old on October 7, 2007 and has continued to enjoy good health throughout her life. Not that it has been an easy life. Is there such a thing? To know Ann and to know her life journey is to be inspired. She's as natural and down-to-earth as any soul could ever be!

Mrs. O'Neill's story is one that will be told over and over again, just as all good stories are. It's a true story of a real mother's love for her daughter.

Mrs. Felixena Phelps O'Neill at Paca Street House, Baltimore MD. Taken November 6, 2007 by MHT. Mrs. O'Neill turned 85 on January 9, 2008.

Mother Seton's story of a soul on the road to sainthood began August 28, 1774, the day she was born. Not that sainthood didn't arrive on January 4, 1821, the day Mother Seton died, but canonization (September 14, 1975) made it official. Canonizations are never for the soul being honored. They are for the glory of God, recognized in the faithfulness of the creatures God has made from love, for love.

When Mrs. O'Neill implored her own dear mother to "Get to the saints!" I can so easily imagine such a meeting in heaven: that Mrs. Phelps, (Mrs. O'Neill's mother), in God's loving presence, simply approached Mother Seton on behalf of her daughter and granddaughter and a plan was put in action. Just as fortuitously, Sr. Mary Alice Fowler approached Mrs. Felixena O'Neill in St. Agnes Hospital, Baltimore, one special Easter Sunday in 1952.

To God be the glory.

This particular chapter was written November 16, 2007, and revised March 17, 2008. The first draft of this book was completed March 19, 2008, and the final writing was finished on August 11, 2008.

The following chapters were previously published by the author:

Chapter Five:
"First World Celebration of Feast of America's Own Saint" *The Catholic Sun*, Syracuse, NY. December 24-31, 1975; pg. 6.

Chapter Seven:
"An Ecumenical Friendship: St. Elizabeth Seton's Philadelphia Friend" *The Catholic Standard and Times*, Philadelphia PA. Vol. 85, No. 18/1; January 4, 1979; pg. 2.

Chapter Nine:
"Nun Sees TV Stars Acting Like Saints" *Empire Magazine: Syracuse Herald-American*, Syracuse, NY. December 7, 1980; pg. 21-25.

Chapter Twelve:
"The Only American-born Saint" *The Catholic Sun*, Syracuse, NY. September 14-20, 1995; pg. 15.

Footnotes of Importance

Sr. Regina Bechtel, SC of the New York Sisters of Charity, located in the Bronx, shared the following dates regarding the establishment of the various communities all related to their holy foundress, St. Elizabeth Ann Seton: 1817 and 1829 mark the years when the New York and Cincinnati missions respectively were begun from the Emmitsburg (1809) community. It was the New York congregation (independent since 12/31/1846) that sent sisters to Halifax in 1849 and sent two sisters to be the leaders of the new community in Convent Station in 1859. The Cincinnati congregation (independent since 3/25/1852) sent sisters to begin a new, independent community in Greensburg in 1870. The dates when each congregation became an independent community are: Emmitsburg (1809), New York (1846), Cincinnati (1852), Halifax (1856), Convent Station (1859), and Greensburg (1870).

Sr. Betty Ann McNeil, D.C. of Emmitsburg shared with me (us) the following information: The Seton foundation of the Sisters of Charity of Saint Joseph's at Emmitsburg is the root for 6 communities of religious women, including the Daughters of Charity, which presently has five USA provinces. Elizabeth Ann Seton is not of foundress of the American parochial school system. Neither the mountain parish of St. Mary's on the Hill, nor St. Joseph's parish in the village of Emmitsburg sponsored or governed St. Joseph's Academy and Free School, which was opened and sponsored solely by the Sisters of Charity of St. Joseph's.

It is unrelated that John Dubois became the third superior of the sisters after the Academy/Free School began. Certainly, he was supportive and involved, but in his role as ecclesiastical superior, not pastor. St. Joseph's Academy and Free School, begun in 1810, was **the first free Catholic school** *for girls, staffed by religious women* in the country. The school was governed, funded, and administered by the Sisters of Charity, who admitted girls from the environs as well as boarders living at a great distance, even as far away as New York and Philadelphia. From the onset, it was *not* a parish school.

Parochial schools got their start later in the century, circa 1852, through **John Neumann** (1811-1860), 4th bishop of Philadelphia, who was a strong advocate of parochial schools. [Of note here is that I had belonged to the Sisters of St. Francis, Syracuse, NY and our "mother foundress", Mother Bernadine Dorn, was invested in the habit of St. Francis by St. John Neumann.] At the time of Neumann's death, the *Metropolitan Catholic Almanac and Laity's Directory* listed thirty-seven parochial schools in his diocese.

Bishop Neuman participated in the deliberations of the First Plenary Council of Baltimore (1852) and served on the Committee for the Education of Catholic Youth. The **First Plenary Council of Baltimore** urged the establishment of parish free schools and pledged to finance them with Church revenue. Building on the educational foundations in existence, the bishops adopted an expanded vision of Catholic education and decreed the creation of the parochial school system in the United States.

Sister further clarified that the Daughters of Charity no not use the term "convent", but live in houses or residences. The Daughters are not religious and use a unique nomenclature. Finally, in reference to Mother Seton calling or referring to the Community Cemetery as "God's Little Acre," Sr. Betty Ann reports there is no extant writing documenting that Elizabeth Ann Seton ever called the cemetery, "God's Little Acre." It appears to be a 19th century fabrication by someone.

I am deeply gratified to the many who have contributed to this collection of stories. Thank you, one and all. God bless us, everyone.

"May the most just, the most high, and the most amiable will of God be accomplished forever."

Breinigsville, PA USA
04 December 2009

228633BV00002B/51/P